Schools
without
counselors

Guidance practices for teachers

Schools
without
counselors

Nelson-Hall Company

Chicago

Guidance
practices
for teachers

William B. Stafford, Ed. D.
Lehigh University

Professional / Technical
Series

ISBN 0–911012–52–4

Library of Congress Catalog Card Number 73–90567

Manufactured in the United States of America.

For
Debbie and Mark

Contents

Contents

viii

Preface

This book is written with a specific purpose and to a specific audience, namely, the elementary school teacher in the school where there is no formalized elementary guidance program, and where there is only a remote chance that there ever will be such a program.

Elementary school teachers are a dedicated lot, who have created much of the enthusiasm of the recent movement of elementary school guidance. Many teachers with whom I have talked have expressed interest in a guidance program, but have added that they see little prospect of such a program under the direction of an elementary counselor becoming a reality in their own school.

The topics in this book have been directed to the questions most commonly raised by teachers about elementary school guidance. The book is brief because it is directed to the issues which teachers felt were the most pressing. In this respect it is not intended to be comprehensive, nor is it written with the intent of making a counselor of the teacher who reads it.

This book is essentially nontechnical and nontheoretical in its format, as it is written with an eye for the practical everyday applications the typical classroom teacher might employ. It offers no pat answers, because it is written with the recognition that complex issues cannot be solved by simple solutions. Indeed, it may raise more questions than it answers.

It does, however, deal with issues and questions related to the elementary school setting. It is hoped that these questions will not be misinterpreted as criticism of or lack of respect for the teacher and the school, as this has not been the intent. At the same time, some of the issues which are dealt with are sensitive areas which require our attention.

The book then, is written for the teachers who are the bedrock foundation of all education, the elementary school teachers. It is written with gratitude, respect, and appreciation for those won-

derful teachers whom I have known personally and professionally, and, equally,
those who have touched and left indelible
impressions upon the lives of my children.

Schools
without
counselors

Guidance practices for teachers

1

An overview of elementary guidance

A BRIEF BACKGROUND

The decade of the 60s was a restive period for education. Since mankind's entrance into the space age and the era of concern for a full and meaningful education for all children regardless of race or ethnic background, the public's attention to the schools changed. This was a change from passive indifference to varying degrees of concern as to how to insure children the finest educational experience possible.

The motives for change were both altruistic and practical. There was a recognition of concern and responsibility for children from less fortunate backgrounds and a striving to find new ways of rectifying old grievances and providing new hope for a fuller and more meaningful life. There were likewise the practical concerns of dealing with the national fear, brought about by the space age, that somehow our schools were not working as well as they should. That is, the schools were not identifying and developing the necessary talent to meet the demands of this new age of man.

Of particular interest here is one manifestation of this phenomenon of concern, namely, the emergence of the movement of counseling and guidance in the elementary school.

Counseling and guidance at the elementary school level was not a phenomenon of the 1960s. It has a long and undistinguished history dating back to the 1920s, when William Burnham (1926), considered by many to be the father of elementary counseling and guidance, made his first pronouncements concerning the need for guidance in the elementary schools. In spite of Burnham's early efforts, elementary guidance became entangled in curriculum reform of the day and was virtually lost as a viable movement.

The reasons for the re-emergence of

elementary school guidance in the 1960s are clear. There was a recognition that the greatest of all of our national resources is the hope and promise of our young people. This in itself is not a new notion, but it is a concept of which, periodically, on a national level we have needed to be reminded.

The very notion of our national security is closely linked to the importance we attach to our young people. That is, if we are to excel, or perhaps survive, as a major nation in the contemporary world, we must take steps to insure that our nation produces enough technologists, scientists, mathematicians, and leaders in various fields of endeavor. In order to achieve these ends, the obvious approach is to identify, at as early an age as possible, those young people who show promise of talents in the desired areas, so that their talents may be fostered, nurtured, encouraged, and developed. Herein lies the assurance of a continuing national dominance.

Whenever the national concern is sufficiently aroused, one of the normal solutions is some form of federal legislation. The above circumstances were no different. In 1964 the National Defense and Education Act was amended, giving the United States Office of Education authority to initiate guidelines for the preparation of counselors in the elementary schools.

Surveys reported by Faust (1968) during this time indicated that during the 1965–66 school year a total of 42,350 elementary school counselors would be needed to achieve a minimum ratio of one counselor to every 600 students. Further projections indicated that by the 1969–70 school year a total of approximately 53,000 elementary school counselors would be needed to achieve the same minimal student/counselor ratio. (1968, p. 65)

With the passage of the amended N. D. E. A. of 1964, the first elementary guidance institutes were established at Arizona State University, University of Illinois, and the University of Missouri. The purpose of the institutes was to recruit promising candidates from the teaching ranks who, upon completion of the institute, would return to their home school, where they would be hired as elementary school counselors. The notion was that the schools would recommend those teachers whom they felt would be competent counselors in their school system, would grant them a leave for further education at government expense, and would accept the newly trained counselors back into the schools as full-time counselors.

When these neophyte institutes were announced to the teaching profession, there was an overwhelming response of applications. Faust (1968) for example, reports that at Arizona State University some 1,800 teachers applied for the thirty available spaces in the institute. He cautions, however, that these rather impressive figures should not mislead the reader to believe that the "Age of Elementary Guidance" had arrived. The sobering fact was that of the 1,800 applicants only thirty-eight could provide convincing evidence that they would be hired by their school systems as full-time counselors upon successful completion of the institute program. When this issue was pursued even further with school administrators, only twenty of the original 1,800 had really firm offers of full-time employment as counselors. (1968, p. 67)

In 1965, the Congress of the United States intervened once again and authorized legislation to subsidize school districts employing elementary school counselors. Thus, the schools were provided with counseling services at the elementary school level with little direct cost to the local taxpayer.

In 1966 Oregon State University established an institute for elementary school counselors similar to those at Arizona, Missouri, and Illinois. This time, when the announcement went out to teachers interested in applying to the institute, nearly 4,000 replied and more than 1,000 were able to present firm commitments of employment as full-time elementary school counselors upon completion of the institute. Faust, the intrepid historian of elementary school guidance, candidly observed the situation as follows:

> Much as professional counselors and counselor educators might like to believe that the sudden new market during 1966 for elementary school counselors was a product of the public schools wishing to enhance the quality of the curriculum, this seems an idealistic interpretation. The flood of federal funds, made available to the school districts, created the market. (1968. p. 70)

The slow progress of elementary school guidance

While there have been many gains made since the first institutes, progress has been surprisingly slow. When one considers the rather high degree of support given to the program, particularly by the federal government, then consideration should be given to the factors impeding the development of the movement.

Certainly the "tax bite" has been a

major factor in both rural and urban schools. This will undoubtedly remain an impediment to the growth of not only elementary guidance, but also to education in general until some realignment is achieved in the existing tax structure and in the methods and procedures of school financing.

It would be invalid, however, to state that the slow progress of the development of elementary school guidance is due entirely to the financial situation. Both the schools and the public have had reservations concerning the appropriateness of counseling and guidance in the elementary schools for a variety of reasons. Some of the more commonly stated objections have included:

1. "There is a greater need for other specialized services within the school, e.g., school psychologists, psychometrists, nurses, reading specialists, curriculum coordinators, and even full-time principals." It is difficult to equate these different types of staff members since each serves a different function within the school. The charge, however, does suggest the need for a careful analysis of the needs of the school and how these needs can best be fulfilled. Other services which may

have a higher priority within the school take precedence over an elementary school counselor. Where resources are limited, however, any additions should be considered in terms of the greatest service to the greatest number to be served.

2. "Elementary school children are too young to have problems requiring the help of a counselor." This charge is difficult to respond to since it typically implies that the person making the charge fails to understand both the nature of children and the function of elementary counseling and guidance. Anyone who knows children and who has worked with them knows that some children exist in situations which would test the mettle of many adults. Likewise, those who make these charges tend to see elementary counseling and guidance in too constrictive a role. That is, they tend to see elementary counselors functioning as "massagers of the child's psyche," as one critic has put it, rather than being concerned with the facilitation of the normal developmental concerns which all children face.

3. "Guiding children is the function of

parents, and elementary school counselors have no right to usurp this function." A charge of this nature displays a misunderstanding of the role of the elementary counselor. Elementary counselors are not concerned with usurping the parents' role, but rather with working with the parents to enhance the child's development. Under favorable conditions the elementary counselor can help to enrich the parent-child relationship through his understanding of child development and the objective point of view he can bring to a given parent-child situation. The counselor is not competing with the parent, but is attempting to work in harmony with both parent and child.

4. "We never had counselors in elementary school when I was a child, and I grew up all right." This statement is also difficult to respond to. It shows, once again, a lack of understanding of the child and the milieu in which he functions. Even young parents of school age children need no expert to remind them of the many social-cultural-technological changes since their own childhood. At the very least, many of the

supports which were present then for both adults and children alike have changed dramatically in the ensuing years. While children, like their parents, may "grow up all right" the purpose of elementary counseling and guidance is to assist the child in finding a fuller and more meaningful life.

5. "We have never really understood the function of the counselor at the secondary level, and there is little need to introduce such an untried program in the elementary school, particularly if the elementary program is to be a duplicate of the secondary program." This point deals with a very real concern, namely the objectives of counseling and guidance at either the elementary or secondary school level. The counseling and guidance programs at the secondary level have a longer and more continuous history than they do at elementary school level. The role and the purpose at the secondary level have been difficult to define to the public for many reasons. Perhaps one of the most difficult aspects has been the lack of concrete examples of what is accomplished as compared to other aspects of the

school. That is, there are no grades or credits at the end of a term to indicate the student's progress and there is no victory or defeat as there is in an interscholastic athletic contest. Additionally, the criterion by which many secondary guidance programs have been judged, right or wrong, has been the number of graduates who go on to institutions of higher education. Certainly, this is an inappropriate criterion for elementary school guidance. There is also the problem that many secondary schools have done an inadequate job of defining the role of counseling and guidance to their many publics, with the result that the counseling and guidance function has remained a great unknown. While a number of varying objectives for counseling and guidance at the elementary school level have been presented by a variety of proponents, the most pertinent and basic goals are involved with the objectives and concerns of the individual school. In brief, the program must have specific goals and purposes for the particular school where the program is being initiated. Carefully thought out objectives for the counseling and guidance function may have the unsettling effect of forcing the school to scrutinize its own over-all educational objectives as well. These goals must not only be well thought out, but must be fully explained and discussed with all who are affected by this program. Certainly an elementary guidance program which is instituted only because of an urge to keep up with the institutional Joneses in the neighboring school is doomed to almost certain failure from the outset. Unfortunately, this has been the case in a number of instances.

6. "Teachers have always been handling the guidance functions within the classroom and there is no need to bring in a counselor." This book is directed primarily at this last objection. Many capable teachers have been and are providing guidance services within the classroom. Even when a fully developed guidance program exists within an elementary school, this does not mean the guidance function is removed from the classroom but that teacher and counselor can combine efforts

to perform this function more effectively.

Guidance is often thought of in terms of a counselor in a one-to-one relationship with a student. While this is one of the functions of a formalized guidance program, guidance in the elementary school is more than this. Elementary guidance is a set of attitudes as well as functions, a process rather than an event, and an understanding which must permeate everyone involved in the education of the child, from the parent to the cafeteria worker, from the principal to the school crossing guard, from the school secretary to the school board member, from the teacher to the building custodian.

Perhaps the effect of attitudes can best be explained through a variety of examples. Compare, if you will, two kindergartens. In one, the children sit quiet and orderly doing the assigned tasks of the teacher. When asked what her objectives are for this group of children, she replies: "My goal for the children is that they will learn to sit still, be quiet, and take orders." In another kindergarten, one need not even ask the question of goals when he views a group of youngsters busy at a variety of tasks, moving around from activity

The influence of adults

13

to activity and seeking the assistance of their peers and their teacher in accomplishing their tasks. Here it is obvious the goal is that the children discover, interact, and learn. As a friend once commented, "many of us need to consider the derivation of the word *kindergarten,* and, perhaps, even more basic, the meaning of *kinder!*"

Again at the kindergarten level, try to imagine the full impact upon a group of young children polished and scrubbed, happy and excited approaching the school for the first day, when a secretary rushes excitedly from the office flailing her arms at the approaching mothers and children and shouting, "Back! Back! The children are not to be in the building for another ten minutes!" As the children's hands clench their mother's and they retreat to the safety of the mother's skirts, one cannot help but speculate on the puzzlement of the teacher at the shyness and quietness of the children when these same children are finally delivered to the confines of her class ten minutes later.

Or, consider the cafeteria server who finds her job an economic must, but who has a low tolerance for noise, who becomes overtly annoyed with the child when he asks her to omit the vegetable dish he dislikes, and who remembers with resentment that she did not even have hot lunches when she was a child in school. Also consider the impatience of the school bus driver who is running behind schedule, when the children dawdle as they board the bus. The list could continue indefinitely.

Everyone encounters an occasional annoyance, of course, but the point being made is the importance of the pervasive attitude that exists throughout the school. Perhaps it can be best determined by the following questions. For whom do the regulations, policies, practices, and goals really exist? For the convenience of the teachers? The administrator? The clerical staff? The custodial staff? The children?

The purpose of the rules and practices offers a key to attitudes. Does the classroom teacher, for example, insist on absolute quiet in the classroom because she feels this is what is expected of her, and that this is an empirical sign that learning is taking place? Or is the balance of order in the classroom dictated by the activity being pursued within the bounds of normal expectations for children's behavior? Does the principal insist that the children march double file on the right side of the corridor at all times in the interest of safety, or because visitors in the building will recognize that he is "run-

15

ning a tight ship"? Would a member of the clerical staff summarily dismiss a child's request because it interrupted her routine, merely because it was a child who made the request, while going out of her way to respond to an identical request from an adult?

The important consideration is the attitude on which the rules are based although one certainly follows the other. In too many situations dealing with children one senses that we follow many practices out of habit after long ago forgetting the reasons for these practices. Many of the practices remain because we were told this is the way it should be, and we observed the practices even though our own private deeper understandings told us we were responding inappropriately. There are many indications that we have lost sight of the fact that children are individuals in their own right and deserve to be respected as such. Unfortunately, in our time many who try to show respect for a child as an individual are charged with the vague and often meaningless crime of being permissive, which has become the ultimate derogation of those who work with children and youth.

What is being advocated here is not the once fashionable child-dominated atmosphere of a few decades ago, where little effort was exerted to correct or direct the child for fear of bruising his psyche. A plea is being made, however, for a valuing of the child where he is in his own stage of development and the recognition of his dignity as an individual.

What is being suggested is that for maximum development of the child there must be a balance of responsibility, expectations, and structure. Children need structure in what they do. Children impose structure on themselves, most noticeably in their play, when they establish limits and rules. They do this to avoid disorder and chaos and to make meaning of what they are doing, just as adults do. But again, there must be balance. With too much structure externally imposed, the child is robbed of initiative and behaves in a robotlike manner.

We, as adults, can and do influence the direction in which the child develops. We do not understand this influence fully, but even in our state of not understanding, we continue to serve as an influence. To the extent that we do know how we influence behavior, we must also know the direction in which we wish to guide this development.

Morris Haimowitz (1966) poses this question in a most penetrating article, "What Kind of People Do We Want?"

where he challenges us to truly question our goals, and the behaviors we exhibit to achieve these goals, in terms of both desirability and consistency.

The appearance of an elementary school counselor on the scene does not assure any change in attitudes on the part of all of those who are concerned in the educational process of the child. The counselor can only be a facilitator in this direction. It has even been suggested that the presence of the counselor may work in reverse. As Arthur Combs has observed at the secondary level:

> When our schools became larger and more complex we invented the counselor to look after the needs of students. And, when this was done, we as teachers felt this was no longer our obligation because, after all, this was now in the hands of the experts. (1968)

The attitudes of understanding and real concern for the children must be present long before a counselor comes into the school if the counselor's presence is to cause anything significant to take place. Research is quite adequate at this point to indicate that for the full development of the child to occur the conditions of acceptance, trust, respect, and faith in the child must be present and must be perceived by the child. These conditions can be met with or without a counselor.

The reader is cautioned that these attitudes are deceptively easy to mention, and far more difficult to fully understand or implement. Perhaps the undergirding principles behind these attitudes are patience and consistency. Too often, where the novice attempts to establish conditions of acceptance and trust in the classroom, she expects to determine for herself if they are practical by the immediate results. The results on a one-trial basis may often be disappointing, or even worse, threatening to the teacher, to the point that she decides the whole notion is too idealistic and resolves she will not risk a second trial.

Perhaps the problem here is that we have been exposed too much to the examples of scientific models. We have learned to expect that through the combination of two parts hydrogen and one part oxygen we have the recognizable compound of water. The human condition, however, is neither that exact nor that stable. There have been prior influences upon the individual, and there are other conditions over which we have little or no control at the present, which may produce end results entirely different from those anticipated.

19

If we are to truly risk ourselves in this endeavor of attempting to more fully achieve the maximum development of the child who sits before us in the classroom, we must be prepared to accept frustration and disappointment as we try to convey our acceptance, trust, respect, and faith to the child. Only as he grows to accept our attitudes as being genuine and dependable will full development be forthcoming.

SUMMARY

To the teacher who believes the basic premise that the child in the elementary school has inner motivation for learning as well as for essentially constructive social behavior, what follows in this book may have some meaning in terms of releasing a potential which needs external freedom and encouragement to flourish. Contrastingly, those who do not view the child's behavior in this manner, but who feel that learning and social behavior must constantly be externally directed, will undoubtedly find what follows to be unacceptable, inappropriate, and perhaps a bit foolish.

The author feels that with the presence of a capable counselor in the school, there is a source of assistance to those teachers who recognize some of the problems briefly sketched here. This is an admitted bias. For a variety of reasons some schools will not have the assistance of a trained counselor for some time to come, if indeed, ever. There still exists a shortage of trained elementary counselors, and there are other priorities which will usurp any funds which might be available for the employment of a counselor. Many of these are often legitimate priorities which should take precedence over the hiring of a counselor, for the presence of a trained counselor will not resolve all the issues of assisting children in their development toward effective adulthood.

What follows will hopefully be of assistance to the classroom teachers or principals who share concern as to how we can more effectively foster and develop the process of learning and growing through the elementary school years.

2

Standardized evaluation procedures

INTRODUCTION

Standardized testing has paralleled the guidance and counseling movement from their respective beginnings. Both were new movements at the turn of the century. Frank Parsons, considered to be the father of guidance, was operating out of his Vocational Bureau in Boston in the early 1900s. At about the same time Alfred Binet was developing the first intelligence test in France in his work with children in the schools.

Binet's work was brought to the United States, where it underwent extensive revision by Lewis M. Terman, who, while on the faculty at Stanford University, published the Stanford Revision of the Binet Intelligence Test, or as it is more commonly referred to, the Stanford-Binet Intelligence Test.

Intelligence testing was devised at the outset to find those children in school who were incapable of profiting from the normal school experience, and who needed special educational attention. As the intelligence test underwent additional changes, broader applications for its use in the school became more apparent.

Similarly, as the purposes of the Vocational Bureau expanded and the guidance counselor became part of the school staff, it was quite natural that the guidance counselor came to rely upon the intelligence tests, and other tests which had also been developed, as some of his primary tools.

For a period of time the "marriage" of testing to the guidance movement appeared to be a good match. As time went on, however, the advisability of the union was increasingly called into question. The primary issues were the exaggerated claims being made for standardized testing, and the decisions which were being made based upon the test results.

Classroom evaluation has also had its share of difficulties, some of which appear to be closely related to the model advanced by standardized testing. While both standardized testing and classroom evaluation have been of concern to guidance and counseling, they are extremely broad topics for consideration. This chapter will deal with standardized testing and the following chapter will be concerned with classroom evaluation.

STANDARDIZED TESTS

No veteran teacher needs to be told that standardized tests have been both the boon and the bane of education. When wisely chosen and intelligently used they can add another dimension of understanding the child in the educational setting. When the choice of tests is questionable and the use based on incomplete information, standardized tests can be misleading, misunderstood, and in some instances destructive.

The story is told, and is presumably true, of a midwestern elementary teacher who was having a conference with a child's mother. The child was achieving at a low level, and the teacher was perplexed when she noted on the child's cumulative record his I.Q. was 142. Even a novice in testing recognized an I.Q. of 142 as well above average. The measured intelligence and the child's achievement were at such complete odds the teacher called the guidance counselor for assistance in explaining this disparity. The counselor, learned and experienced in the ways of standardized testing, was equally confused at the disparity between the I.Q. test score and the child's achievement, until he suddenly noticed that the 142 was indeed not the I.Q. for the child, but rather, the number of days the child had been present in school the prior year!

Similar errors have been reported by hundreds, and bear no further repetition here. They do serve to indicate the extreme caution called for in the use and interpretation of all such standardized tests.

Notwithstanding the possible problems, it should be recognized that standardized tests are a part of the educational structure in our country, for the present time at least. They are suggested, recommended, subsidized, or mandated by state and federal bodies, by various educational and professional organizations and even by parent groups. Since tests are being used it becomes necessary to find the most intelligent and meaningful manner in which to utilize the results of these tests.

Test selection

Methods of test selection will vary not only from community to community, but from school to school as well. Test selection can be based on a program devised or recommended by the superintendent, the principal, the building administrator, the head teacher, the school psychologist, the school counselor, a testing committee, the individual teacher, or combinations of these groups. In some instances, it has even been observed that officials of varying capacities at the secondary level have planned elementary testing programs without the advice and consent of the elementary staff and with very little understanding of the purpose of testing in the elementary school. This method of planning invites chaos and the misuse of standardized tests.

No matter who makes the selections of the tests, there are a variety of factors which need to be considered in making the choice.

What information is really needed and provided by the test? It needs to be recognized at the outset there is nothing magical about standardized tests. They are specifically devised tools to tap into and to provide certain types of information. The overriding question here is whether the test really provides the data desired, and whether this is the most effective way of obtaining this data. Or, perhaps put a

27

different way, what will be known after the testing that isn't already known, and is it information that is needed for some constructive and useful purpose?

A number of generally reliable and satisfactory instruments are available on the market at the present time for assessment in a number of areas of concern to the educator. The question remains as to what the results of these tests tell, and equally as important, what they do not tell.

For the sake of brevity, let us deal here with the intelligence test. What the intelligence test provides is an *approximation* of where the child was in his overall intellectual development at the time the test was administered. It is only an approximation because of factors related to the test itself and factors related to the child's status at the time he took the test. In the former instance, tests will vary in their ability to assess that elusive quality we call intelligence. The design of the test itself may also have characteristics which make the test confusing to the child who takes it. Some examples of this will be given in later sections of this chapter.

In terms of factors related to the child which may affect the test, the list is almost endless. Was the child in good health? Did the child just receive a scolding from the teacher? Did he just have a tiff with his best friend? Was the purpose of the test clear, or was he anxious or upset about the possible results? These and other factors all play an important role in the child's performance on the test.

What the test does not give us is an absolute and irrefutable evaluation of the child's ability. It is, as stated, an approximation. It may or may not indicate the ceiling of the child's abilities, since we can never know whether the child is functioning at peak performance. It does not reveal the innate abilities of the child, for no test yet devised claims such omnipotence. It may or it may not predict what the child's abilities will be x years hence. In the early elementary years particularly, children's measured abilities show remarkable changes due to factors related to the growth and development of the child, the variety of experiences the child encounters, and the freedom he has to explore these experiences.

Where does this leave us in terms of the meaning of the test? If we need an approximate assessment of the child's ability for the purpose of working more effectively with the child the standardized test may be of assistance to us. It may also provide us with some additional clues concerning areas which are in need of additional investigation related to the child's functioning. The standardized test, however, should *never* be taken as the final pronouncement that it measures the full extent of the child's ability.

How will we utilize test information? At the risk of oversimplifying the issue, one particular aspect will be examined. In a number of schools across the country it is deemed educationally sound to administer reading tests periodically to children in the elementary schools. While, basically, no one would argue with this practice, in many situations the testing is an exercise in futility in that it is only half a program. Where there are no resources, nor any immediate prospects for resources, to provide special services to those who need assistance, we identify "slow readers" with no prospect of really helping the children. The children who are "diagnosed" with no immediate prospect of assistance may become increasingly anxious now that they have been told they are in difficulty, as may those most concerned with the children and their progress.

This is not to suggest that we take an ostrichlike posture and ignore learning difficulties of whatever nature. It does suggest, however, that testing should be considered·in a list of priorities. In some instances a half a loaf may be worse than no loaf at all.

How appropriate is the test for the particular school? Perhaps it is safe to say that one of the greatest misuses of tests lies in that they may be inappropriate for a particular school. As has been suggested earlier, there are a myriad of tests devised for some highly specific purposes. There should be as close a fit as possible between the objectives of the test and the objectives of the school.

While numerous examples could be cited to exemplify this point, a glaring example might be seen in a standardized test created to measure the progress of elementary school children in the so-called modern math. It would be quite inappropriate to use a test designed to measure these skills with a group taught in the more "traditional" math skills since different approaches, techniques, problems, and methods of solving problems are involved in the modern math.

While so great a disparity between the objectives of testing and teaching may appear to be quite obvious to the reader there are far more subtle differences which may show up. Take, for example, an elementary school which administered to its students each year the Iowa Test of Basic Skills, in which one of the subtests is concerned with the mechanics of English (i.e., capitalization, punctuation, and spelling). The school decided that during a particular year they wanted to emphasize written expression in a more creative fashion. In order to achieve this goal, the school placed less emphasis on the mechanics of English. And so the experimental program was implemented. When the test results came back from the I. T. B. S., the scores for the mechanics of English section were significantly lower than on other parts of the test, as well as lower than they had been on the same test in previous years. In this deliberate trade-off of creativity at the expense of mechanics no one was distraught, since the results were anticipated from the outset. Had similar results been obtained in other circumstances, the interpretation would have been different and the results, perhaps, far more disconcerting.

For any meaningful evaluation of the child, the class, or the school, there must be a close alignment between the objectives of the curriculum and the objectives of the test. To assume that because a test which has a good reputation nationally will also be appropriate for a given school is folly. It cannot be overstressed that the two objectives, those of the school curriculum and the test, must be in harmony if meaningful results are to be obtained.

Are we getting the most for our money in using this particular test? This question is concerned essentially with an ordering of priorities of time, money, personnel, and facilities of a given school. It is important to determine where we can put existing educational resources to maximize effectiveness. We must make such decisions as whether to use our resources for one good test for which there exist the personnel and facilities to work with the information obtained or whether to experiment with a "shotgun approach" to give information in a variety of areas, and hope that we can successfully cope with and constructively utilize the data obtained.

Where resources are limited, another question which certainly must be asked is whether the resources available can be put to more effective use in working with the children in areas other than testing. If resources are limited, and the use of tests within the school is justified primarily by reasoning that it is educationally "the thing to do," then perhaps a reordering of priorities is needed. By regrouping resources and attending to recognized problem areas, perhaps both diagnosis and remediation can be better accomplished in a given area. Perhaps we should abandon the notion of more testing and focus instead on gaining maximum benefits from a few well chosen tests, complemented by programs which can follow through and utilize the information obtained for the betterment of the children involved.

The use of tests for grouping

The notion of developing programs for the betterment of children deserves a closer look and perhaps redefinition on the part of all of us who are concerned with the development of the child. We can no longer justify the use of tests for purposes of traditional grouping or categorization of the child. In too many instances this grouping has been done for administrative convenience, in response to the teachers' cry that it is impossible to teach the full range of talents and abilities one finds in the normal classroom. Claims have also been made that children will function more effectively when placed in homogenous groups. That is, in advanced groups, without the slower children holding the better students back, the more talented students will progress more rapidly. Following the same line of thinking, the contention has also been advanced that slower children will also advance more effectively when taken out of competition with the more able students. In either event the research evidence has been sadly lacking to substantiate any con-

vincing argument for grouping. While there are other reasons, perhaps the following three critical reasons are why grouping based on standardized testing has failed to achieve what was anticipated.
1. We have continually misunderstood one of the critical concepts behind testing, namely that measured characteristics are *not* fixed and immutable. Standardized test results cannot be viewed as a final characterization of a child any more than one would categorize as final a child's height or weight at any given measurement. Evaluation of the fact that Eddie weighs 75 pounds at a given weigh-in is dependent on a variety of factors. Certainly his age and height would be two variables to consider. It would be most unusual, however, with an elementary child, to say that Eddie weighs 75 pounds and then resign ourselves to the fact that he will always weigh 75 pounds.

The same variation exists in all measurable human characteristics. We expect change as the child progresses in age. While we can accept this with characteristics such as height, weight, maturity of judgment, etc., however, we have a tendency to view academic abilities (math, spelling, punctuation, even I.Q.) as being somehow different, and to see that once we measure a child's abilities they somehow will become arrested from any further development. As is true of height, weight, and maturity of judgment, the whole spectrum of human abilities develops at different rates at different times in each individual.

2. A second area of confusion and difficulty in grouping has come about perhaps because of the term "grouping" itself. Grouping implies putting together a number of people who share common characteristics. In a teachers' lounge one very commonly hears a colleague state that he must get ready for his "slow group" or "fast group." One's imagination forms a picture of a classroom of look-alikes with either very dull or very eager faces depending upon which group one refers to.

The only time you will have a completely homogenous group is when you have a group of one. The only safe assumption we can make about the individuals in the group is that they shared some *generally* common characteristics at the time the group was first formed, whether by teacher evaluation or by standardized test results. We have no assurance, however, that the group was or is monolithic in nature.

In addition, no matter how similar the

group may have been at the time of its creation, there is nothing to support the notion that they will share these common abilities to the same extent at any future time. Elementary school children in particular, because of their rapid and variable rate of growth, will remain at the same level for a very short period of time. We, therefore, run the very real risk of impeding the child's growth if we label him "slow" and assign him to a "slow group." The same may also be true of the "bright" student. By placing him in the "advanced" section, we can run the risk of making demands which may be too rigid and which may detract from other aspects of his over-all growth and development which to him are as important as academic achievement.

Probably one of the most commonly heard phrases in education is "individual differences." It is also probably the most ignored concept in actual practice. No matter how carefully chosen the group may have been at the outset, there will still be as much variation among the children as there are members of the group and, perhaps, as much variation within each individual child as there are numbers of days the child meets in the class.

3. Finally, an additional consideration we must recognize in grouping as it is

normally structured, is that the groups tend to validate notions the student may have of himself. The group, if you will, tends to put the final seal of approval on the abilities of the child. It makes little difference if we use the labels of "Red Bird," "Blue Bird," "Group I," "Group V," or the more direct labels of "High Ability" and "Remedial." The child discovers in little time where he has been categorized. Most students rather quickly adjust to this labeling and perform in accordance to the expectations of the teachers. (Rosenthal and Jacobson, 1968) It is particularly devastating how quickly, and apparently permanently, children learn to fail. (Kagan and Moss, 1962)

These criticisms of traditional groups do not suggest there is no other alternative but traditional heterogenous grouping. There are a number of alternatives which can be explored and which suggest ways of using test data.

While our purpose here is not to promote a particular curriculum approach, one brief example may be helpful.

When children take an achievement test it is rare that the child will make consistent scores on all sub-tests. That is, he may score high in arithmetic and lower in language. We would anticipate that the majority of children would show some variations in ability. The probable exceptions would be the very bright or very slow students, but even here one would anticipate some variation.

If the test scores are further validated by the teacher's observations then relatively minor adjustments allow the possibility of providing a real opportunity for the child's growth without the normal stereotyping of the child's development.

One such procedure, which is increasingly being used, is to ungrade subject areas. That is, the major subject areas are examined for levels of achievement at the various grade levels. If a child is low in language skills for his age group and high in arithmetic for his age group, he is allowed to float to the level of his competence. He might, as a fourth grade student, be functioning at a second grade reading level and a fifth grade arithmetic level. By allowing him to float we are being more realistic in terms of his growth. This does require careful and continual assessment on the part of the teacher so that when he is ready to move up or down in any particular area the means for accomplishing this floating are available and are not circumscribed by grading periods, semesters, or years.

Scoring errors

All too frequently, even in those situations where tests have been chosen with a great deal of care and understanding of the tests, money saving measures are undertaken at a critical step, scoring. The veteran elementary teacher who has escaped hand scoring standardized group tests is indeed unique.

Hand scoring. Hand scoring 25 to 35 sets of group tests is monotonous, routine, and boring. While one can sympathize with the teacher because of the drudgery involved, more important is the factor of human error which enters into the final results of the tests due to the monotony of the scoring process. Some school systems employ teacher aids or older students to score tests to save the teacher from the drudgery of this task. The end results may be equally disastrous. An incorrectly scored test is not only useless, but dangerous. Hand scoring tests to avoid the extra cost of having them machine scored and running the risk of more error in the process is obviously practicing false economy, especially when one considers the use to which test scores are typically put.

If a test is worth giving for the information it will yield, it is worth taking care each step of the way to assure the obtaining of the most accurate results possible. In most instances, this negates the practice of hand scoring.

Machine scoring. Even where machine scoring is utilized, however, the test user must not be lulled into unquestioning acceptance of test results. Scoring machines must basically be programmed by humans, and therefore are capable, at the first step, of human error. Cases have been reported of disparity of test results when the same test was scored on repeated occasions by a machine scoring service. (Burack, 1961; Weigel, Roehlke, and Poe, 1965; Merwin, Bradley, Johnson, and John, 1965) While the many corporations who machine score standardized tests are constantly striving to increase their accuracy, the alert teacher will not place unquestioning faith in test results, but will keep an alert eye for obvious and inexplicable deviations, so that tests can be rescored or interpreted with greater caution if the results are suspect.

Recording scores. Care should also be taken to insure the accurate recording of test scores in the student's cumulative record. This, once again, is one of those routine clerical tasks which invites error because of the monotony of the task involved. The example cited earlier of the child's prior attendance record being recorded as his intelligence quotient may be somewhat rare, but the inaccurate copying of scores from the test answer sheet to the cumulative record is, unfortunately, not a rare occurrence.

There are, of course, ways to avoid errors. Companies who score tests are increasingly using individual score reports with an adhesive on the back side. These labels normally contain the student's name, the name of the test, the date when the test was taken, and the child's scores. The labels can be affixed directly to the child's cumulative record, thus eliminating transcription errors. While there is usually an additional cost for these test score labels, the cost is comparable to clerical costs for transcribing the scores. Also, in terms of accurate score reporting there is no comparison.

Where the school feels the additional cost for test score labels cannot be justified, an alternate method of reducing the transcription error is, of course, the process of double checking the results once they have been entered into the student's cumulative record. While this process increases the accuracy of the transcription process, the same problems of routine and boredom are still present, and errors may still be made. Again, because of the importance typically attached to test results, even one error in transcription of the test scores calls for a more accurate system of recording.

Other sources of error

While a virtually endless list of possible sources of error in standardized testing could be presented, two areas which are of particular importance at the elementary school level need to be considered.

On intelligence tests and on some achievement tests the child's age, often in terms of months, is requested and is used in routine scoring procedures. These tests are designed with the idea that the older child should be able to perform more difficult tasks. Any inaccuracies in reporting the child's age will drastically alter the final score and the meaning of the test. In most situations, the child enters his age on the answer sheet himself and for a host of reasons it may be inaccurate. An error of even a few months can significantly alter the typical child's test results and, of course, the resulting interpretations and uses of the information. For this reason the age entered on the answer sheet should be carefully checked before the test is scored.

Another source of error with which we should be concerned is the type of answer sheet used in standardized testing.

The answer sheets can cause problems in two ways.

Particularly on achievement tests, which are composed of a variety of sub-tests dealing with subject areas, young children have a tendency to become confused and mark their answers in the wrong section of the answer sheet. This appears to be particularly true when the testing covers an extended period of time, as is typical of most achievement tests.

While test designers and publishers have done a great deal in the actual design of the test to avoid this problem, it still occurs, particularly when test fatigue begins to set in, when the testing is extended over a period of several days and when tests are not taken in sequential order. Thus, the child may be taking the math sub-test, but marking his answers in the English usage part of the answer sheet. If this goes undetected, only chance responses in both sections will be scored correctly. When such an error occurs, the test gives no measure of the child's abilities in either area, and any diagnostic value of the test is entirely lost. Errors in the marking of answer sheets occur often enough to warrant the teacher's careful proctoring of the students while they are taking the test to be sure the students are marking responses on the correct section of the answer sheet.

Answer sheets designed for young children may present another problem in the manner in which children are asked to mark their responses. The typical answer sheet generally uses one of three styles.

FIGURE 1   Three typical styles of marking responses.

Vertical dotted lines

A B C D

Horizontal dotted lines

A = = = =
B = = = =
C = = = =
D = = = =

Circles

A B C D
o o o o

There is some evidence to suggest that elementary children, because of their physical immaturity, have more trouble with the physiologically more difficult vertical motion demanded by dotted lines. As a result, particularly in a timed test, the children may be penalized, and the test results may be more of a function of physiological development than actual knowledge related to the test. Girls may have an advantage over boys in a test using this type of answer sheet because of

45

their typically more advanced physiological development.

Information about tests

It is beyond the scope and intent of this book to go into specific details concerning all the tests which might be appropriate to the elementary school setting. There are, however, areas which need our consideration and attention in the selection, interpretation, and utilization of test results.

The obvious source to turn to for an understanding of a test is the manual which accompanies all reputable tests. The author and publisher of the test provide a description of the test, what it purports to measure, and how well it achieves this task, along with additional information which should be helpful in understanding and interpreting the test results. This source of information is critical for learning both what the test is and what it measures. It should not, however, be viewed as the final authority or the only source of information about the test. Test authors and publishers may see their instrument in a different perspective than the prospective user, because of their involvement with the particular instrument, and may, unwittingly, fail to see the weaknesses of the test. Also, it must be remembered that test publishers are selling a product. As in any other form of marketing, the salesman wants to present his merchandise—the test—in its best possible light.

Those who work with tests generally acknowledge four general categories of tests, even though there is some lack of agreement concerning these categories.

Aptitude tests. This is a rather conglomerate category, and probably the category which encompasses the greatest differences of opinion among those who are familiar with testing. Over-all aptitude tests may be of a general nature or quite specific in terms of special aptitudes.

The general aptitude test is concerned with an evaluation of the individual's over-all ability, and is typically representative of the types of measures we call an intelligence test. The aptitude test attempts to measure the individual's ability to perform. An aptitude test may also measure quite specific aptitudes in such areas as art, music, computational skills, mechanical abilities, etc. The tests may vary from traditional paper and pencil tests to tests involving such activities as manipulating objects and discriminating tone and pitch.

As has been suggested, aptitude tests are among the more controversial tests because the distinction between aptitude and achievement has not been defined or conceptualized clearly enough. Aptitude tests have historically been believed to somehow measure innate characteristics, and, indeed, there are those who still hold this notion. In even the best formulated arguments it is exceedingly difficult to separate what one was born with and what one has learned. The result has been that the distinctions between aptitude and achievement tests have not been as clear as they were once held to be.

Achievement tests. While some distinctions between aptitude and achievement tests were mentioned in the prior section, the primary function of an achievement test is to measure the individual's acquired knowledge. Typically, achievement tests come in a battery form and measure the individual's knowledge and understandings in a number of academic subject areas. The Iowa Tests of Basic Skills and the Metropolitan Achievement Tests are two rather common examples of achievement tests.

An additional characteristic of the achievement test, in contrast with the aptitude test, is that the achievement test should reflect dramatic changes in a particular area in which the student has developed new insights, understandings, and interest. For example, if a child in the fourth grade who had achieved at the fiftieth percentile on the arithmetic sub-test suddenly took a new interest in and gained new understandings of arithmetic to the point he involved himself much of the time on working mathematical problems, we would expect a higher score on his arithmetic sub-test the next time he took the achievement test. This is the very nature of the achievement test. A general aptitude test would theoretically not reflect such a dramatic change; on the other hand, a specific aptitude test dealing with mathematical skills would undoubtedly reflect this growth.

Interest tests. Interest tests are used for vocational and career planning. The basic rationale behind interest tests is to compare the student's indicated interests with the interests of those who are functioning in various careers. The groups of interests indicated by the student are related either to specific occupations and careers or to broad areas of similarly related occupations and careers. Interest tests are concerned solely with the interests of the child, and they do not take into consideration any skills or abilities the child may have.

The use of interest tests at the elementary school level is questionable at best. Research indicates quite clearly that career choice, as is true of most other human characteristics, is an evolving, maturing process. The child's interests, even in the upper elementary grades, is so temporary that their assessment has extremely limited value to either the child or the school.

Personality tests. Personality tests come in a variety of formats. There are personality tests calling for both group and individual types of administration, and tests dealing with clinical diagnosis or in terms of strengths of particular characteristics of the individual. In their basic format, most tests are paper and pencil tests, where the individual typically responds that each descriptive statement contained in the instrument "is descriptive of me," "does not describe me," or "I am uncertain whether this applies to me." Other personality tests may use pictures or designs which the individual responds to verbally by describing what the picture or design suggests to him.

Personality tests are held in high regard by some and are thoroughly criticized by others. The only area of even tentative agreement between the advocates and critics of personality tests is that their use is only safe and possibly productive when they are being used by a trained and experienced professional.

The mass use of personality tests,

with the possible exception of their use for research purposes, is held in very low regard. Some states have prohibited mass use of personality tests by law, and typically parental permission is required in writing prior to the administration of any such test.

In brief, the use of personality tests in the elementary school is highly questionable and when they are used at all they clearly should be in the hands of highly trained professionals.

Probably the best known and most widely used outside reference of standardized tests is the *Mental Measurements Yearbook*. (Buros, 1969) This publication contains descriptive information concerning tests which are currently available on the market. Additionally, this book contains reviews and critiques of the tests by various researchers who have utilized and examined the tests in a variety of situations. This book is an extremely valuable source of information to the individual school planning to use a given test for particular purposes.

Tests in Print (1961), also by Buros, provides an effective description of tests which are currently available on the market, but it does not have the extensive reviews and critiques of the *Mental Measurements Yearbook*.

Other books which were essentially designed as textbooks in the area of testing provide some information concerning the various tests available. Equally important, these books contain more detailed information concerning test selection and interpretation and the utilization of standardized test information. The reader is referred to such sources as Super and Crites (1962), Goldman (1961), and Cronbach (1970). Additional information is available in the various professional journals dealing with testing.

Information from sources such as these is needed by the individual or group responsible for the selection of any standardized test, so that choices may be made with the most complete information it is possible to accumulate. In addition, this information should be readily available to each classroom teacher so that she is fully aware of what the test can and cannot do, how she can use the results most effectively in working with children, and so that she is better prepared to interpret the test results to whoever is deemed appropriate.

Interpretation of test results

Each step along the path of standardized testing has its own peculiar problems, and the area of interpretation of test results is no different. Certainly a test score standing alone has very limited meaning. There are some basic understandings which must be paired with the test score for it to have any significance. The two most important are an understanding of the child and an understanding of the test.

Norms. Norms show how different representative groups perform on a particular test. While these norms are helpful in understanding test results, they are only an approximate representation of the group with which the individual teacher is working. While there are many similarities to the group the teacher is concerned with, there will also probably be differences of either a direct or subtle nature. There may be local customs, traditions, values, standards, and practices which may make the local population unique enough to be divergent from the larger norming sample. For the most effective group interpretation of test scores, local norms should be established and continually developed, always with a critical eye for changes in the population and resulting changes in the way in which children perform.

It is important to understand what the norms tell us. There seems to be a prevailing notion that in terms of ability or achievement one must score above average, and in terms of personality and adjustment one must score at the average. The whole notion of the normal distribution curve makes these notions untenable. Tests are designed to discriminate among individuals; thus it is inevitable, and inherent in the design of tests, that some will score in the low range, some in the average range, and some in the above average range. Tests which do not present a distribution of scores are of little or no value. Taking the distribution into consideration we must gain a clearer understanding of what a low score, an average score, or a high score mean.

Meaningful test interpretation is not predicated on a single test, nor should any attempt be made to pigeonhole an individual on a single test. A single test score has the value only of showing where a given individual was at the time when he took that test. A far better understanding of the meaning of a test score is obtained when the test is one in a sequential pattern of tests. An understanding of growth, consolidation, or regression on the part of the individual can be obtained when the series of scores is viewed in the context of the sequential developmental pattern of tests.

Test scores can be viewed much more realistically by looking at them as a part of a pattern of developmental growth, or lack of it, rather than merely observing that on a given test the student scored at a given percentile ranking. An illustration may be helpful here. Assume a school gives the Iowa Tests of Basic Skills to Children starting in the third grade and tests them in the fall of each subsequent year. Figure 2 (page 56) shows a hypothetical representation of a student's score based upon national norms.

From Figure 2 a number of observations can be made. The most critical factor is that change did occur at each grade level when the testing took place. There are indications of growth (see reading, language, and work study skills), regression (see vocabulary between third and fourth grade), and consolidation (see arithmetic). Since the above represents a hypothetical student we can speculate freely concerning the causes of the changes in the test scores. How much more realistic and exciting if we knew the student and were able to see some of the causes for these changes!

We can also speculate at the way the information would be received by the student or the student's parents that instead of merely being below average in his test scores that he made some gains, encountered some losses (perhaps at the expense

FIGURE 2   Hypothetical representation of a student's score.

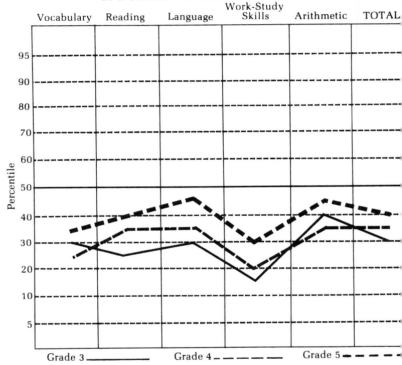

of the gains?), and went through some consolidation in terms of his measured abilities.

Through viewing test scores in this fashion the emphasis changes from comparing the student with wide representative samples of children his age to making the comparison that counts most, namely with his own past growth.

We must make a shift in our thinking in terms of ways that we view test results. If our goal is to bring everybody up to an average or above average score on any type of aptitude or achievement test, we are doomed to frustration and failure. The closest analogy, perhaps, is attempting to place everyone in a classroom in the top half of that class in terms of academic achievement. It is logically inconsistent to attempt such a feat. It is, additionally, misleading, naive, and self-defeating to promise students and their parents that this can be accomplished in our present educational structure. And yet, to a certain extent, we often make such claims. When we are unable to make good on these claims we needlessly make students and their parents feel guilty and frustrated. In addition, we ourselves lose the confidence and support of the public, because we have not delivered on our promises.

Far more realistic is the goal of seeing growth and development from one point to another. Norms are helpful in viewing this progress in that they give us a common yardstick by which to measure students. If we can move from this measurement to the next step of viewing the individual's growth, we have data far more meaningful, and far more helpful in working with students.

The use of norms is, of course, related to the application of mathematical concepts in testing. Measures in terms of centrality, stanines, percentiles, standard deviations, T scores, z scores, etc. have traditionally appeared too arcane to many readers or have aroused the reaction that "math always was difficult for me." The fact is that testing and mathematical concepts have been closely interwoven since the beginning of the testing movement as we know it today.

While this book will not go into the mathematical concepts on which tests are based, the reader is referred to Leona Tyler's book, *Tests and Measurements* (Tyler, 1963), which is written in a highly readable fashion, for a basic explanation of these concepts.

For the purposes of this discussion, however, there are two basic concepts which it is important for us to understand. One is the normal distribution curve, and the other is the standard error of measurement.

Normal distribution curve. The concept behind the normal distribution curve preceded the testing movement as we know it today. At the same time, it has been an integral part of standardized testing since its very beginnings.

The basic notion behind the normal distribution curve is simply that any trait measured on a broad and representative population, when graphed, will distribute itself in a predictable fashion. This notion had long been an accepted notion in mathematics and science in terms of predicting probability. In the nineteenth century, however, a Belgian statistician by the name of Adolphe Quételet demonstrated that this notion could also be applied to the measurement of human traits. Quételet took the height and weight measurements of a regiment of French soldiers. In instances of both height and weight he found that the majority of soldiers had the same or nearly the same height or weight, and that those deviating in either direction from the average, i.e., the extremely tall or extremely short, were by far fewer in number. In fact, Quételet determined that it could be predicted what percentage of the population of soldiers would be average in height, what percentage would be below average in height, and what percentage would be above average in height.

When Quételet plotted the height of

the French soldiers on a graph, he found that a pattern, similar to Figure 3, emerged.

Unfortunately, Quételet felt that, among other findings, his graphs suggested that the average range represented the ideal toward which Nature was working, and that deviations, i.e., the very tall and the very short, were in fact undesirable mutations of Nature's grand plan. To some extent this line of reasoning prevails today, as was suggested earlier in relation to scores on personality and adjustment tests.

FIGURE 3   A normal distribution curve showing the distribution of height of the French soldiers measured by Quételet.

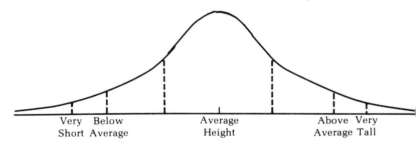

The importance of Quételet's findings was that they were based on an application of a principle already well accepted in mathematics and science; but applied for the first time in terms of human characteristics. Quételet's findings gained greater importance when they came under the scrutiny of, and influenced the later work of Sir Francis Galton, who is known today as the father of mental testing. (Goodenough, 1950)

The significance, then, of the normal distribution curve for our consideration is:

1) If a broad and representative enough sample of subjects is used in measurement of human abilities, when plotted on a graph they will distribute themselves in a predictable manner, which we recognize as the normal distribution curve. It can be observed from Figure 4 below, for example, that 68.26 percent of a given population will score in the so-called average range on a given test (34.13 + 34.13 = 68.26). Likewise, 2.27 percent will score either in the very high or the very low range of the test (2.14 + .13 = 2.27).

The breadth and representativeness of the group cannot be overstressed in terms of scores, traits, or characteristics being represented on a normal distribution curve. Local norms, which were previously mentioned, would not normally be characterized by the normal distribution curve because a somewhat restricted population would tend to lack the full range of abilities. This is not to rule out the possibility of a normal curve occurring in some large systems where data would be collected over an extensive period of time, but the probability remains quite limited.

FIGURE 4   The normal distribution curve.

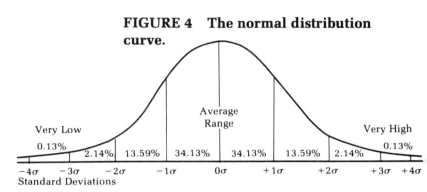

2) Test authors design their instrument to fit the normal distribution curve. Assuming the test is valid and reliable, that is that it measures what it claims to measure, and that it is consistent in its results, the test author knows that if the test is given to the whole spectrum of a population, the scores will distribute themselves in a range similar to that shown in Figure 4 above. Typically, a new instrument is field tested with a representative sample of the population. If the results are diverse enough to suggest a normal distribution through this sample

testing, the test author "normalizes" his findings to fit the model of the normal distribution curve.

3) An understanding of the basic notions of the normal distribution curve also lends understanding, as we will see directly, in the consideration of the standard error of measurement.

Standard deviation. Closely related to an understanding of the normal distribution curve is a grasp of the statistical concept of standard deviation. Again, for purposes intended here, no statistical computations will be considered. Our concern will lie with what the standard deviation is.

Briefly stated, the standard deviation represents how, on the average, a group of test scores deviate from the over-all average of scores in a given distribution. Where the scores are drawn from the full spectrum of a given total population, we would expect the scores to fall at four standard deviations on either side of the mean, or the average, of the total distribution, as shown in Figure 4. To the right of the mean are positive deviations, represented by $+1\sigma$, $+2\sigma$, etc. The symbol following the number (σ) is the lower-case Greek letter for sigma, which represents the standard deviation. The plus sign indicates the deviations are higher than the mean. Likewise, to the left of the mean the numbers are preceded by a negative sign $(-)$, indicating these deviations are less than the mean.

For each test a numerical value can be determined for both the mean and the standard deviation, based on a number of factors such as the range of scores (highest to lowest scores), how the group who took the test performed, the appropriateness of the test for the group, etc.

Referring again to the normal distribution curve in Figure 4, assume the mean score equals 100, and that after computation the standard deviation is found to equal 10. We know then that by adding 10 to the mean and each subsequent standard deviation we would have the values:

$$+ 1\sigma = 110$$
$$+ 2\sigma = 120$$
$$+ 3\sigma = 130$$
$$+ 4\sigma = 140$$

and that by subtracting 10 from the mean and each subsequent standard deviation we would have the values:

$$- 1\sigma = 90$$
$$- 2\sigma = 80$$
$$- 3\sigma = 70$$
$$- 4\sigma = 60$$

Further, based on prior discussion of the normal distribution curve, we know that approximately ⅔ of the population (68.26 percent, which represents that part of the population scoring between -1σ and $+1\sigma$) will achieve a score between 90 and 110.

This general concept of the standard deviation is not only helpful in visualizing test scores more clearly, but it is also important in understanding the standard error of measurement, which follows.

Standard error of measurement. The folly and danger of accepting a single test score as being a fixed, immutable, and final classification of a person's abilities has been discussed throughout this chapter. Numerous reasons have been given as to why this is inadvisable. Still another reason deserves our attention: namely the effect of the standard error of measurement.

Psychometrists and test authors have long recognized that if the same person repeated the same test several times there would be fluctuations in the scores the person would make which would be due to factors other than his familiarity with the test. There are a number of factors which can and do influence the way a person performs on a given test. The physical and emotional well-being of the student, the physical conditions of the testing room (temperature, light, comfort of working conditions, distractions, etc.), the style and temperament of the examiner, the "test taking sophistication" of the student, and the test itself are but a few of the variables which can and do affect the way in which a person performs.

The standard error of measurement, then, is a statistical means of determining what the probable error of measurement for a given test is, which in turn provides the user with a further means of refining and understanding the results of the test with which he is working.

Let us take a hypothetical example to see how this works. Let us say that student *A* takes a test in mathematical achievement and he makes a score of 115. Presented on a graph that includes other students of the same age and similar educational background, we see his score as in Figure 5.

FIGURE 5   Student *A*'s score of 115.

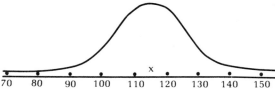

If, through the calculation of the standard error of measurement, we find it has a value of 5, we note that it too is plotted on a normal type curve (see Figure 6).

FIGURE 6

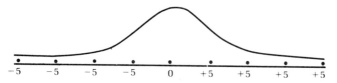

Superimposing this on the larger distribution containing *A*'s score, we obtain the curves in Figure 7.

FIGURE 7

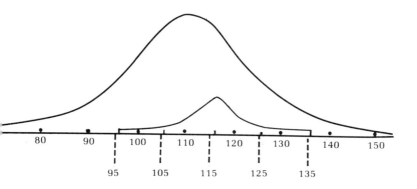

While Figure 7 is somewhat exaggerated for purposes of illustration, it can be noted that 68.26 percent of the time A would make a score between 110 and 120. In other words, two out of three times we would expect A's score to fall into this range. This probable range is far more meaningful than a single score of 115, and with the assurance the score will fall into this range two out of three times, one has a far more reliable score with which to work. Many test publishers are now utilizing this method in the reporting of scores, and the scores are usually represented in a manner similar to Figure 8.

FIGURE 8

Raw score			Percentile scores
	130	98	
	120	84	
	110	50	
	100	15	
	90	2	
	80	1	

Should scores be interpreted to parents and children?

An issue which has perplexed educators for a number of years is whether test scores should be made known to parents and children. A number of distinguished educators have argued the pros and cons of the issue over the years. The N.E.A.

Journal (Fenner, 1961) garnered a group of knowledgeable and distinguished educators and psychologists in the field to discuss both the merits and difficulties of interpreting test scores to those outside the profession. *Test Service Bulletin* (Seashore, 1959) also has discussed this issue as have a variety of other publications. While there are valid considerations on both sides of the issue, one of the most important questions is how we get the full value of tests without utilizing the results as fully as possible.

There is much to suggest that rather than operating by rigid policy, schools should use a bit of common sense in dealing with the issue. An example may be helpful. Parents of an elementary school child were having an interview with a school principal concerning the progress of their child in school. The father was a Ph.D. psychologist with a respected reputation in his profession. The mother was a trained and practicing psychometrist, equally recognized and respected in her profession. During the course of the conversation, the principal acknowledged that an intelligence test had been administered to their child, but that school policy did not permit him to discuss the results because they were too complicated for parents to understand.

While not all parents are psychologists and psychometrists, a school that has information which could be of value in helping the child, and withholds that information, is violating its own rationale for being. There probably is no other area of information concerning the child in the school in which information is concealed from the parents in this manner.

Many schools take the attitude that parents will misuse or misunderstand the information. While this may often be true, we, as educators, must share some part of the responsibility for not better informing the parents of the children whom we teach so they can use this information constructively.

It has often seemed strange that a student's full test profile at the secondary school level will be released to a college admissions office, and yet be unavailable to the student or the parent. Test records are also sent when they are requested by the courts, prospective employers, and others outside the school. Many of the people to whom test profiles will be sent have little or no training in psychometrics. It is interesting and frightening to speculate that if the psychologist father mentioned previously had instead been a shop owner, he could have obtained with little difficulty the scores which he as a parent had been denied, merely on the basis of hiring his own child.

Even more important, under most circumstances the agency receiving test data has no idea whatsoever of the purpose and the intent or the use of the tests in question. It may have no knowledge of whether they were administered because of a persuasive test salesman, whether one pressure group or another brought their use into existence, or whether they were part of a carefully conceived plan of pupil evaluation. Equally important, as has been suggested earlier, are the questions of how the tests were scored, what norms were used, and what were the testing conditions.

In recent years the giving out of test scores and other information about the student has been viewed from a new perspective. A growing concern has emerged that the schools have been too willing to share test data and other personal information with outside agencies and individuals. The result has been that those speaking for the child have felt the child's right to privacy has been breached. A number of recommendations concerning safeguards to the child's right to privacy have been made outlining levels of information about the child, who may have access to this information, and under what circumstances this information may be released. A rather comprehensive look at the problems involved and tentative proposals for dealing with this situation have been covered in a publication prepared by the Russell Sage Foundation. (Goslin, 1969)

The issue of whether test scores should be shared with parents and children is too complex to be settled here. However, where the scores are to be given to the family, the consideration of the following suggestions should make the information more valuable to them.

Know the purpose of the test. While this and other comments which will follow may sound redundant, at the same time these are most significant considerations for use in test interpretation. If the test has been carefully planned for and has a specific purpose in the educational scheme of the school, then its purpose should have meaning and importance for both parent and child. The score ceases then to be a meaningless number to be politely discussed and forgotten or an added bit of misunderstood conversation. If there is no clear purpose for the test, if it is a case of "we have always given this test and continue to do so," then in all probability the results will have little meaning for parent, child, or teacher and may even be more confusing than enlightening.

Know the test. Knowing the test is different than knowing the purpose of the test. The conscientious teacher who is involved in the establishment of the testing program will know the strengths and weaknesses of the test and its evaluation not only by author and publisher, but by other reviewers as well, and will be able to discuss the test intelligently and meaningfully with both students and parents.

Know the population. In order to communicate anything meaningful the teacher must know both the student and parent population. This means more than a generalized notion about the "parent group" and the "student group"; it means knowing that Johnny becomes dejected when he knows he has not done as well as his friends, that Mary's father is a very exacting individual who will exert undue demands on Mary to "bring those scores up the next time," or that Tom's father and mother did not go beyond the eighth grade, and while they are interested in Tom's progress, they may have difficulty in understanding test results and their meaning.

Present the data clearly. How will the test scores be most clearly presented?

There is no pat answer, of course, since it depends upon the skill of the teacher and the ability, mentally and emotionally, of the parents and students to understand. Percentiles may be one of the basic ways of explaining test scores, as most parents are readily able to understand that "out of every one hundred similar children who took this test, your child scored as such and such a point." Again, however, merely reciting statistics is only one step in the process.

Explain what the scores really mean. As has been stated the single most important aspect in test interpretation is the notion of growth, consolidation, or regression. This, after all, is the primary consideration for testing. It has been said earlier that no one would consider the single measurement of height or weight at any given period of a child's life as *his* height or *his* weight; so it should be for standardized testing. When each succeeding test is taken, the score should provide us with new information which, when added to prior test data, allows us to form a more complete picture of the growing and developing child. In this way test data can be used to assist the child in further growth and development rather than merely to compare him against the average of the norm group.

Finally, another aspect which needs to be emphasized in explaining and interpreting test scores is the fact that a test is a sample of behavior at a single fixed time. A test score may represent nothing more than this. It has been suggested earlier that a variety of factors may influence test results at any given time. Great caution should therefore be used in dealing with any singular test score and, perhaps rather than relying on a single test score the same test should be repeated periodically in order to gain a more accurate and comprehensive understanding of the child. Hopefully, with some understanding of the limitations of test scores, we will see an end of such labeling as "underachiever" and even worse, "overachiever." Both of these labels present a constricted view of test scores and suggest an omniscience through testing which is just not there.

A classic example of the misuse of the scores of standardized testing is reported by Hoffman, a strong critic of testing abuse, who reports the following incident:

In a school in one of the largest cities in the United States, a young girl had been doing very nicely in slow regular classes in the third, fourth, and fifth grade with three successive teachers. In the fifth grade she was at the top of her class. Yet the school psychologist, discovering that the student's I.Q. was below 70, had her taken out of the class in which she was doing so well and placed in a class for mentally retarded children. Nor is this all. When the fifth-grade teacher complained, the assistant principal told her that performance did not count—only the I.Q. counted. Nor is even this all. The teacher brought the matter to the attention of leading figures in the world of testing and received virtually unanimous letters strongly condemning the action of the school psychologist in ignoring actual school performance and relying instead on the I.Q., especially since the girl's native language was not English—a fact of which the school psychologist was well aware. The teacher showed these powerful letters to the school principal, and the principal agreed that the student had done very well in her regular fifth-grade class —but he backed the psychologist. And he in turn was backed by higher authorities. (1962, p. 111–12)

CONCLUSION

While one might be tempted to take a firm position either supporting the use of tests in the educational structure or condemning the use of these devices altogether, testing is currently firmly entrenched in the schools and is unlikely to be abandoned. The best course, then, is to find the most productive and meaningful way in which to use the test results.

If we attempt to use test scores to set up various remedial programs with the ultimate goal of bringing everyone up to average, we are engaged in a self-defeating and futile process. The very nature of the statistical and norming concepts indicates to us this cannot be accomplished. If we totally accept the premise of the statistical and norming processes, on the other hand, then we may reason that the child is inevitably ranked where he is within the group and nothing can be done. Certainly, for many teachers this alternative is also unacceptable.

Perhaps an acceptable alternative is to reconsider some of the basic elements of our educational structure, determining how the school can facilitate the growth and development of the child within the school structure without basing their plan on his responses to a standardized achievement test. This alternative begins with a literal subscription to the notion of taking the child where he is and working with him from that point of his development.

Current research suggests that each of us has within himself a genetic clock, so to speak, that determines when and how individual traits will manifest themselves. The notion may be analogous to a group of people taking a trip from one city to another. The method of transportation employed will determine when they arrive at their point of destination. Obviously, the person traveling by jet will get there first. The persons traveling by train, bus, automobile, or by foot will all arrive at different times, but the point is that they will all arrive at the point of destination assuming their mode of transportation does not break down altogether.

By using test results to assist us to see the child more clearly we are in a position to promote the growth and development of the child. But this way of looking at test results will involve fresh insights, a venturesome spirit, and a willingness to face frustration as it is, a break with the traditional ways of dealing with tests. The overriding question seems to be whether we feel the typical current practices concerning testing are so inadequate that change must come about, or whether we feel the risks of a different approach and a different use of tests are so great that we must not abandon present practices in spite of any shortcomings we may sense in the present system.

3

Evaluation
procedures
in the classroom

Evaluation in the classroom is a formidable task. Certainly any teacher who is sensitive to her students feels some frustration when she attempts to reduce the sum total of their efforts over a given period of time to either a letter grade or a numerical grade which is supposed to be an adequate representation of the student's efforts and accomplishments. This frustration often centers on two basic questions of *what* we are doing in evaluation, and *how* we are doing it. While there are no universal answers to the problem of classroom evaluation, we can draw upon the observations, experiences, learnings, and insights of a variety of individuals, which perhaps provide some further understanding of this issue.

Some years ago a colleague likened all evaluation to the way they weigh hogs in Texas. According to his story, when a Texan wants to weigh a hog, he takes the hog to a field. There he takes a wooden plank and balances it on a large rock. Then he places the hog on one end and on the other end he places rocks he finds in the field, until the hog and the rocks balance one another. Then the farmer guesses the weight of the rocks and he has the weight of the hog!

In the same way all of us engaged in education have perhaps persuaded ourselves that when we are giving a grade we have a precise measurement of what an individual student has done in the classroom when in reality we may have been guessing the weight of rocks.

There is at least a partial explanation of why we have been so willing to accept this notion of precision. During this century, education has become involved in a questionable "numbers game" that began when two Frenchmen devised the first intelligence test. Even though these two pioneers, Binet and Simon, as well as many of those who followed them in this area of endeavor, constantly admonished that these scores were only approximations, the public at large, and perhaps the field of education in particular, was eager to accept these scores as an extremely precise evaluation. One historical reviewer (Goodenough, 1950), looking at the power of standardized test results in the mid 1920s, claimed that the public put as much faith in these test results as their fathers had placed in the accuracy of their favorite phrenologist's map. Grades or scores, whether based on the most carefully planned standardized test or the individual teacher's evaluation, are regarded as having the precision and accuracy of the best calibrated yardstick when in reality they may represent an elastic yardstick that can, at best, be considered only an approximation of an evaluation.

In addition to this notion of precision there is a nineteenth-century notion which we would do well to discard still lingering in our thinking. That notion is that the classroom teacher is the paragon of all virtue, all knowledge, and all understanding, and generally is not prone to human frailties. This notion is undoubtedly a carryover from an earlier time, when the "school marm" sought to establish herself and her profession within the community. We must divest ourselves of this image, not only as it relates to evaluation, as we will examine here, but also as it relates to the teacher's interactions with the child and the parents, which will be discussed in a later section.

What constitutes a grade?

While on the surface it may seem simple to ask what constitutes a child's grade in a course, further examination may reveal that the question is not as simple as it seems. For example, is the child's grade merely a reflection of what he has achieved academically over a period of time, or does it include "nonacademic" considerations as well?

If it does include "nonacademic" aspects this may lead us to question the legitimacy of including in the grade evaluation the child receives these variables having nothing to do with the child's academic performance in class. Much of what is involved in the grading process will depend upon what the school, and more realistically what the teacher, feels is a legitimate basis for a grade. Even where the composition of the grade is defined by the school, individual teacher interpretation will enter in. For example, if the school maintains that "attitude is a part of the grade evaluation," what then will we include under attitude? Attitude in class as it relates to the particular subject area?

Over-all school attitude? Will it also include some of the fringe areas such as the child's reported out of school behavior or personal characteristics of the child? Finally, we are faced with the question of how will we justify their inclusion or exclusion on the student's evaluation. When we evaluate conduct, we consider not only specific incidents but also the general more pervasive attitude the child conveys. What we should consider is what the mix of conduct and achievement is that constitutes the grade, whether we are aware of it when we make the grade evaluation, and, above all, whether our mix is legitimate. At issue is the cause and effect relationship between the student's attitudes, characteristics, or traits and the way they influence the student's academic evaluation.

We may be, consciously or unconsciously, sent on a "witch hunt" for flaws in a child because of some attitude, characteristic, or trait the child has which we find personally annoying. For example, Joey is the only boy in the fourth grade with long hair. While the school is not happy with Joey's long hair, the school also knows his parents support his decision to wear long hair. Joey also makes lower marks than his teacher feels he is capable of making. His teacher reasons that people with long hair are indifferent to education, and that his indifference is the cause of his poor performance in school. More than Joey's attitude may be involved here; when the teacher evaluates him, her attitude regarding long hair may make her consciously or unconsciously hold Joey more accountable in his studies than boys with more traditional hair styles.

The above example may be so blatant as to be misleading. Take Fred for example. Fred is recognized as a bully on the playground, and he also makes low marks in school. We might do well to question whether Fred makes low marks because he is a bully, or whether Fred is a bully because he makes low marks.

Even as parents have felt annoyed with their child when they have planned some special event for him, only to have it be met with indifference or even rejection because the child, being a child, happened to be interested in something else at that given moment, the teacher also experiences these same feelings. The reactions of parent, child, and teacher are all perfectly normal. The same thing may happen in the class when the teacher has given extra effort for some project in the class which she feels will be of special interest to the students, and she notices Mary gazing out the window, perhaps thinking of the "Jacques Cousteau Special" she watched the night before, or Johnny, who has contained his natural childish enthusiasm as long as he can, pinching the student sitting next to him. Does the teacher see this with the recognition that Mary is thinking of the T.V. special, and that Johnny's pent-up energy must find its release? If the teacher is most remarkable perhaps she does, but more realistically she is likely to be annoyed and angry or even to question her own teaching ability. The question being raised here is whether the teacher puts more into the grade than the straight academic activity of the classroom. Is Johnny's grade only going to be a reflection of what he knows and can relate about the project under discussion, or will his grade also include his behavior in being disrespectful and disrupting the class by trying to pinch the youngster next to him? Are we evaluating conduct, achievement, or both?

One of my former students who is a particularly fine and sensitive teacher, was working with a small group of boys who were classified as mildly disturbed. One day after a class session in which we had discussed behavior modification, he told of some of the behavioral problems he was encountering in his class of boys.

When he was asked for some specifics he cited such behaviors as wandering around and out of class, picking on one another, abusive language, and so forth. He ended by stating he would like to try behavior modification, but he was unsure as to how to start. It was suggested he start by listing the negative behaviors he wanted to extinguish and by keeping a frequency chart for a week's time to see what the frequency of the undesirable behavior was. In this manner he would have a base established to determine if the techniques of modification which he would later employ were actually altering behavior. He agreed to do this and to report his progress the following week. When he returned the following week, he put a paper on the desk which contained the categories of undesirable behavior, but there were no frequencies following the categories.

When he was asked about the absence of frequencies, he stated he had observed the class carefully all week, and none of the behaviors had been exhibited. He had finally concluded that he had been carrying an image in his mind of the way the boys had behaved at the beginning of the school year. Though the boys' behavior had changed, his image of it had not—until he attempted to record the frequencies of their undesirable behavior.

This example demonstrates the very

subtle nature of factors which influence the way we perceive students and their behavior. Certainly the teacher had no malicious intent in this instance, but he did have a very real question of what he was accomplishing with this group of boys. There was no formal evaluation in terms of grades being made of the boys in this instance, but had there been such an evaluation without this examination, it certainly would have been misleading.

The above is not an isolated example by any means. The main issue here is the very subtle nature of the influences which act upon us in making any assessment of human interaction. Many studies have been made in this area. While the two which have been arbitrarily chosen for elaboration do not relate specifically to evaluation in terms of grades, they do deal directly with the general issue involved in giving grades.

Getzels and Jackson (1962) in studying the elusive area of creativity, attempted to separate students into two categories: those who scored high on tests of intelligence and those who scored high on tests of creativity. Getzels and Jackson observed these two divergent groups in a variety of situations to see how they responded and, in turn, to see how others responded to them.

The authors observed that the

teachers ranked those children scoring high in intelligence at the top of the students in the class, i.e., the most desirable students and those who achieved most effectively. Those who scored high on tests of creativity were ranked at about the middle of the class. In some instances the teachers viewed the "creative" children with some degree of annoyance, presumably because these children did the unexpected. While unexpected behavior is an anticipated characteristic of a creative child by most definitions, it is apparently not a desirable trait for the teacher who craves an orderly classroom. The teachers' response to the "creative" children shows an interesting contradiction since most teachers indicate that creativity is a trait they wish to cultivate in children.

A second study, which has been referred to previously, was conducted by Rosenthal and Jacobson (1968).

In this study the prime notion is that of a "self-fulfilling prophecy." While this study has been criticized for some of the research techniques employed, the findings themselves have received support from other areas of research. Rosenthal and Jacobson demonstrated that when teachers were told that specific children would improve academically throughout the school year based on standardized test results, when the children had been randomly selected, the teachers did in fact see improvement in the children. There was often accompanying academic improvement, although not consistently at levels that were statistically significant. In addition, other children who had not been designated to the teachers as ones who would improve throughout the school year, but who in fact did improve, were viewed with some annoyance by the teachers because these students *were not supposed to improve.*

Other sources could also be cited which support the notion that the way the teacher views the child, even when the reasons are not directly related to academic achievement, ultimately finds its way into the academic evaluation of the child.

While we have been looking at the teacher and the influences upon her which can affect her evaluation, it is also important to consider the over-all attitude of the school toward the evaulation of the child. Attitudes stemming from the larger institution of the school can, and do, influence very basic practices in the process of evaluating the child.

One of the factors involved in this consideration is concerned with the absolute standards employed by many schools.

How, for example, have we determined that a grade of 93 is equal to an A, 92 is equal to a B, and so on? Or, how do we determine a student must have an over-all 75 to pass, but that a student who has 74 fails? It is difficult to think of any other aspect of evaluation in life in which so much precision is demanded. Whether it is myth or fact, many automobile drivers feel that they have a five-mile-per-hour margin over the posted speed limit before any action will be taken. Even Ivory soap claims to be only $99^{44}/_{100}$ percent pure in an age of overexaggerated claims for commercial products. In our schools, however, one point can make the difference between passing and failing or between a C and a B.

The meaning of a C grade deserves special consideration. Many schools state on a student's report card that a grade of C is awarded for average achievement, but how much do we really subscribe to this notion? In teacher-parent conferences when the child has been evaluated as doing C work, the teacher's typical comment is that with some more hard work the child can bring the grade up the next time, which seems implicitly to be stating a C in fact is not all right, nor is it average.

One reason for our failure to be satisfied with a C grade is our inability to accept average in the area of achievement. We hope that the child, through additional effort, will achieve beyond this average level. Thus we go back to the statistically improbable desire to put everybody in the top half of the class in every subject.

This lack of acceptance for the average goes beyond the bounds of the school and, to some extent at least, may be an attitude carried from the school. I have an automobile on which the fuel gauge registers "half full" when the tank is full. The attendant at the service station is aware of this malfunction and cautions me that one day I will be stranded because I have run out of fuel. He says this although he knows the fuel gauge registers effectively except that it never goes any higher than half full. Our difference is that he views the malfunctioning of my fuel gauge as an absolute, while I view it in relative terms. The point is that I understand the operation of this gauge and operate my automobile accordingly. As will be shown, the understanding of children's achievement requires the same sort of viewpoint.

The desire to put everybody in the top half of the class is often so serious that it is difficult to examine it objectively. The following "The Animal School" is included in the hope that we might back away from the issue and look at it in a different perspective.

The Animal School

Once upon a time, the animals decided they must do something heroic to meet the problems of A New World. So they organized a school. They adopted an activity curriculum consisting of running, climbing, swimming and flying. To make it easier to administer, all the animals took all the subjects.

The duck was excellent in swimming —better in fact than his instructor—and made passing grades in flying, but he was very poor in running. Since he was slow in running he had to stay after school and also drop swimming to practice running. This was kept up until his web feet were badly worn and he was only average in swimming.

The rabbit started at the top of the class in running but had a nervous breakdown because of so much overwork trying to compete in the swimming area.

The squirrel was excellent in climbing until he developed frustration in the flying class where his teacher made him start from the ground up instead of from the tree-top down.

The eagle was a problem child and was disciplined severely. In the climbing class he beat all the others to the top of the tree but insisted on using his own way to get there.

At the end of the year an abnormal eel that could swim exceedingly well and also run, climb and fly a little had the highest average and was valedictorian.

The prairie dogs stayed out of school and fought the tax levy because the administration would not add digging and burrowing to the curriculum. They apprenticed their children to a badger and later joined the ground hogs and gophers to start a successful private school.*

*G. H. Reavis, "The Animal School," *George H. Reavis: Educator, Editor, Philanthropist* (Bloomington, Indiana: Phi Delta Kappa, Inc., 1971), pp. 10–13.

Grade evaluation and grade distribution go back to the consideration of the normal distribution curve in the previous chapter. While many shy away from any use of statistics, one concept of statistics which has found its way into many classrooms is the notion of "grading on the curve." The grades are deliberately distributed so that a few will make A's in the class, a few will make F's, a larger number will make D's and B's, while the bulk of the students will make C's, the average grade.

While grading on the curve may seem to be logical, and to be supported by sound testing theory, one of the underlying assumptions of the normal curve is that the sample be large enough and inclusive of the full spectrum of abilities. It is most unlikely that any given classroom, or even the same grade level on a city wide basis, would include the full spectrum of abilities. If the normal curve is unlikely to apply to a typical class it is still less likely to fit an "unusual" class of better than average students, or a class which seems less able than usual. When a class has been grouped according to ability, the use of a curve would result in a complete distortion of any meaningful evaluation.

Another question might be raised: "What is our yardstick of evaluation for the child?'' Looking at the typical school setting our answer has to be that we are measuring the child against the progress and achievement of other children in the classroom. If, in fact, this is the case, we have no basis for this practice in terms of what we know of intellectual growth and development. Measuring a child against his classmates will undoubtedly result in a restricted view of the child's learning and his over-all development.

If we look for a rationale to justify comparing the child against his peers for the individual's academic evaluation, we may come away from this experience poor. Our only rationale for such practice is to be found in the area of statistical evaluation which serves the purpose of discriminating among large groups of individuals. The statistical approach utilized in standardized testing and carried over into the classroom is similar to the mechanic's view of the malfunctioning fuel gauge mentioned previously. By his standard it will never be adequate in comparison with fully functioning fuel gauges. While this is accepted as being true, even with a malfunctioning fuel gauge the automobile may travel as far as the other car with the gauge registering full when the fuel tank is full.

If the purpose of evaluation is to measure the child's academic growth, then we must look for a different model than statistical analysis related to standardized testing. The more appropriate model for measurement and evaluation is that of child growth and development, and the recognition of individual differences in the rate of growth. Children grow at different rates and different times. Even children in the same family, with the possible exception of identical twins, have their own timetables for development which show as much variability as there are numbers of people being compared. From the incomplete research data we have, there is little to suggest that intellectual development differs significantly from physical growth and development in its variability.

Willard Olson recognized this individuality of growth rate thirty years ago when he stated:

Teachers should not expect the same effects from the same instruction or from the best adaptation of instruction to the individual. The folly of common expectancies on the part of the teacher, administrator or parent is obvious since achievement is only partially under the control of the educational process. (1944, p. 61)

On the basis of Olson's writings as well as others, we may conclude that we have been using an inappropriate yardstick. That is, instead of measuring the child against the progress of others in the class, we should be measuring the child against himself. Instead of measuring Eddie's progress against that of Tom, Jack, Ellen, and Sue, we should be evaluating Eddie's progress from where he was when we last evaluated him to where he is now, so that we truly get a measure of Eddie's intellectual growth. This, of course, is the essence of what is referred to as the ungraded school. A companion feature of this notion is the nongraded school, which has received a great deal of attention, both pro and con, but with extremely limited practice. In essence the ungraded school is organized so that if a child is working at the equivalent of fourth grade reading and the equivalent of third grade mathematics, the child shifts back and forth between sections for the various subjects. When he is evaluated, however, the child is rated in terms of growth, consolidation, or regression between periods of evaluation, and is moved ahead, held where he is, or moved back based on the development he has shown.

No matter what approach to evaluation is implemented, it is imperative that we understand the process, and that our choice is supported by as much reason and research as we can muster.

Do others know the make-up of the grade?

While some components of the evaluation may be included unwittingly, much of the evaluation is planned. Since grading can include so many factors and weight them in so many different ways, those who are affected or directed by these components of the evaluation should be aware of the components.

As far as the students are concerned, they must have a rather clear notion of the components of the evaluation if we are to hold them accountable for their progress. Are they aware, for example, that turning in work late, being absent from school, and demonstrating unsatisfactory attitudes will all affect the evaluation the teacher makes? If not, one can only share in their bewilderment when, feeling that they did their work adequately, they receive a poor evaluation from their teacher.

Likewise, the parents need to be fully informed of what is expected of their child so they can provide whatever supervision or assistance may be necessary if the child is to progress in his educational achievement. While the parents may not approve of what all is included in the evaluation process, they need to know what is expected of their child if they are to be of assistance to him in the process. Fortunately, in many areas, the days are gone when parents accepted unquestioningly what went on in the school. As a result parents are becoming more aware of their impact and influence on their child in his educational progress. They are also, in some instances, demanding that teachers take a closer look at and question practices such as grading.

Finally, as users of the evaluations, teachers in later grades need to know how the evaluations were determined. It may be argued that as long as the child remains in the same school, colleagues will know how the students were evaluated, so there is no problem. While this line of reasoning could be questioned under the best of circumstances, because of the high mobility of our population, the seemingly never-ending district boundary changes, and the fact that contact between the elementary school and the receiving junior high or the middle school is, in most instances, virtually nonexistent, this argument becomes even more questionable.

In those instances where the child will be going to a junior high or a middle school, or in those situations where it is known the child will be going to another school because his parents are moving, an additional effort should be made to explain the evaluation. Two very basic procedures might be considered. One might be to include a descriptive report of the school and the make-up of the student body with the grades to provide the receiving school some general background of the child's earlier educational experiences. This, of course, could be a duplicated report, which could be revised periodically to reflect changes both in population or philosophy in the school.

The second approach deals more directly with the current discussion. A brief narrative report concerning the particular child's progress would be a most helpful complement to the child's formal evaluative record. While there is always the question of what to include in such a narrative report, perhaps the best response is to include the type of information that would be helpful to you if you were receiving the new student so that you could work with him more effectively.

It is not uncommon for two or more teachers teaching the same grade level to employ entirely different standards in the evaluation of their students. Very minimally this calls for close communication among teachers for at least an understanding of how the grades were determined.

Explaining the evaluation can be a sticky area, because it is sometimes felt that the kinds of evaluations a teacher makes of her students are a reflection of her individual competency as a teacher. In those instances where the teacher makes evaluations with the intent of enhancing her reputation, some children will become lost in the process. The truly effective teacher should have a rather clear notion of what she is doing in the evaluation process, and enough confidence in her own security as a teacher that she can openly discuss methods and standards of evaluation in such a manner that it is of maximum benefit for the development of the child.

It is unfortunately true that in many human endeavors, practices often outlive purposes. That is, originally we have a need or a purpose for developing certain practices. Subsequently, because practices are more tangible than the rationale which spawned them, the practices are often followed long after the purpose has been forgotten. This general pattern of organized human behavior also applies to practices of evaluation. It is not restricted to any

What are the ultimate purposes of evaluation?

103

one level of education, but permeates the entire educational structure.

Certainly there is some cause for us to pause and consider carefully what purposes our grading system serves and how effectively these purposes are being served. In terms of effectiveness it would appear that on a national basis at least, we must conclude our methods of evaluation are found wanting if the goal of the public schools is still to educate the masses. Evidence, which cannot be ignored, is that between 30 and 40 percent of our students, depending upon the source examined, are failed out, dropped out, or pushed out of school, normally by the time they reach the eighth or ninth grade. Obviously, there are a variety of factors, not all of which are directly related to the school, which impede a child's academic development. While it might be argued that evaluation of the student's academic progress is not intended to keep the child in school, it should also follow that evaluations should not be used to remove the child from school. Once again we are faced with the purpose of evaluation and the attendant goals of education. If the primary goal of education is to educate the masses, i.e., to facilitate the maximum growth of every individual, then it seems incongruent to systematically determine that a certain percent of students will not be permitted to continue their educational development. If, on the other hand, we will arbitrarily determine the criteria for achievement by setting minimal standards for achievement, thus terminating certain individuals' academic development based upon achievement, then the procedures mentioned previously are consistent with the goals. There must, however, be a corresponding honesty with those who are affected by such choices.

Because of our inability or unwillingness to deal with this incongruity in the past, we have been in the embarrassing situation of attempting to explain to the various publics of the school why there is such a high drop-out, fail-out, push-out rate in the public schools.

As noted, one of the commonly stated goals of education in this country is the universal education of the populace. In spite of our stated purpose, however, practices in American education, in the main, are still cast in the same mold upon which the earliest educational structures of the United States were founded. The early educational system of this country was not based on an interest in universal education; it was concerned with educating the masses in basic skills, but more important, it was concerned with further educating the gifted males to become the priests of our society, i.e., the physicians, the clergy, the attorneys, etc. The educational system was structured to assure that not everyone would go through the system.

In the course of time educational purposes have changed, at least as far as public pronouncements are concerned. We now view universal education as the means to a fuller life intellectually, socially, and financially. The difficulty, however, lies in the fact that while the public purposes have changed, except for minor modifications the practices have not changed. In some respects the practices have become more rigid.

A resolution of differences between purposes and practices is badly needed. Indeed, the whole system cries out for evaluation and reassessment. Perhaps one of the reasons that the evaluation and assessment have not come about yet is the changing role of the educational leader of the school, the administrator. By force of circumstance, his role has changed from educational leader of the school to building planner and public relations specialist responsible for raising additional revenue to operate the schools. While the importance of these functions cannot be ignored, at the same time the school needs the guidance of an educational leader.

What are some of the results of our current evaluation practices? We have long believed that the grade serves as a further reinforcement for learning. It is suggested here that with the exception of a very few students, this notion is a myth of which we would do well to rid ourselves. Those who will compete for A's in a class are those who feel they have a chance for getting A's, while those who through experience know, or think they know, that they cannot achieve these marks are willing to sit back and watch those who think they can try for the top marks. Someone has compared competition for grades to a college football game, where 30,000 spectators who need the exercise and don't get it, sit and watch 22 people who don't need the exercise get it!

An additional problem with grades is that when we as adults become overconcerned about getting good marks, and when we convey this concern to the child, we may create new problems by making the grade so important that the child will do anything in order to obtain it, with little concern for any learning along the way. It is under these circumstances that the student learns to copy from others' papers, to use crib notes, or whatever other means he can devise to beat the system. The results of this approach are obviously unsatisfactory.

Is the answer, then, to throw out all means of evaluation as some have suggested? No evaluation at all is clearly as equally unsatisfactory. Neither you nor I would care to undergo surgery with a surgeon who was licensed to practice merely because he was dutiful in putting in the prescribed time in medical school.

Some individuals, such as B. F. Skinner (1968), say there is little need for failure if the subject is approached in the proper manner and presented in a more scientific way than it currently is. He strongly advocates learning from results obtained from experimentation in the laboratory to refine the whole teaching-learning process. Skinner's approach is logical and orderly. He emphasizes the need for the teacher to clearly define what is needed to be learned, to carefully analyze in sequential order the various subtasks which need to be acquired which, when combined, will result in the mastery of the more global task originally defined. A key point of Skinner's theory is to positively reinforce the desired skills at each step of the process which leads to the more global task. Skinner's approach has been compared to the building of a wall (global task) with each brick being laid in sequential order to achieve the desired outcome.

Skinner is so confident of this approach that he sees this as not only being practical in terms of teaching academic subjects such as mathematics, science, etc., but that his model is quite appropriate in arranging social cultures. This idea was first presented in a Utopian novel, *Walden Two* (1948), and more recently in a highly successful, but equally controversial book, *Beyond Freedom and Dignity* (1971). Skinner's is but one approach. Others have been suggested, and still others will most assuredly be advanced in time.

If no ideal evaluation system has yet been devised, it is essentially because what evaluation—or indeed education itself—should be achieving has not yet been fully defined nor fully understood. There is, however, one basic principle which must be central to whatever methods of evaluation are ultimately adopted. That principle is that evaluations must be *presented* and *accepted* in such a way that they will facilitate further growth on the part of the child rather than being interpreted by the child as a "put down" for what he has attempted. Before we can even approach this practice, however, we need to deal with the more basic and fundamental question—education for what?

**Other
factors
influencing
personal
and
academic
development**
Earlier in this chapter it has been recognized there are factors outside the school which are potent influences upon the child both personally and academically. Recently Jencks (1972) has brought this issue forcefully to the attention of the public with his best-selling book; many other authors have dealt with the subject as well. The issues involved are complex and varied, with the result that what follows was arbitrarily chosen and makes no pretense of being all-inclusive.

What follows in this section is not intended as a guideline to resolve all problems, but rather as a review of some of the areas to which we need to be resensitized so that perhaps we can at least function more effectively.

Because of the complexity of the issues presented there is no suggestion that if issues are recognized they are immediately capable of being resolved. This "fix them up" attitude has been the source of frustration of the public schools, in that it again represents promises made to a public to deal with issues with which the schools were inadequately staffed to handle and have been incapable of achieving. The public has, as a result, been disillusioned because the schools could not fulfill their promises.

Havighurst in his book, *Growing Up In River City* (1962), looks at a group of children in a longitudinal study covering a span of nine years to see what factors contribute to the success and which to the failure of the child in his growth and development from the age of eleven through the age of twenty. He makes the observation that the child's success in and progress through the school was a good reflection of the child's over-all development from childhood to adulthood. That is, the child who was successful and adapted well in the school had eminently greater chances of being a successful adaptive adult outside the school setting, as opposed to the child whose growth and development in school was not as complete.

While this may appear to be obvious, the reasons for the success or failure may not be what one suspects. Many educators would suggest that the basic intellectual ability of the individual is the essential difference between success and failure, but Havighurst suggests that there appear to be three main factors influential in predicting a child's success: 1) having a good mind, 2) coming from a middle-class home, and 3) having a healthy acceptance of oneself and, in turn, being accepted by others. Havighurst is particularly involved with the role and influence of social forces within an individual's immediate environment as they shape, mold, and develop the child. In addition, he looks at the tremendous influence these social forces have on a number of the skills and attitudes which, when taken collectively, exert an influence on the over-all achievement and development of the individual.

Stated simply, Havighurst is cautioning us that if we focus only on the measured abilities of the child we are looking at only one of those three significant factors which influence the development of the individual. Havighurst does not see the school as the only agency responsible for the fuller development of individuals but suggests all the social agencies (i.e., churches, juvenile agencies, social agencies, youth organizations, etc.) must act in concert. Havighurst places special emphasis on an interaction of these agencies because he recognizes the social forces outside of school, as well as those in the school, which are affecting the individual's development.

It should be noted that when Havighurst looks at the development of the young adult, he does not consider going on to college as the sole criterion of successful development. He looks as well at the young person's opportunity to enter the job market, his success on the job, his ability to stay on the right side of the law, his chances for entering into a successful marriage, and his chances of social mobility.

While it may be argued that Havighurst's book is somewhat dated because of the rapidly changing social milieu of young people, there is still much of value in this book for all who work with children and youth.

Havighurst is not alone in stressing the theme of social influence, nor is he the first to report research in this area. A somewhat similar study preceded his in the book, *Elmtown's Youth* (Hollingshead, 1949). While Hollingshead's study was at a different time and employed a cross-sectional approach rather than the longitudinal approach used by Havighurst, the results were quite similar in that Hollingshead also recognized the importance of social influences upon the individual's development from childhood to adulthood. A particularly penetrating study which was conducted by Davis (1948) was significantly ahead of its time and was, in many respects, prophetic of the current social dilemma in education. Davis examined the motivational structure of the middle- and lower-class cultures and the strong social influences affecting these different motivational structures. In his study, Davis expressed two deep concerns: first, that for the schools, which essentially reflect middle-class standards, to influence the development of children in the lower-class culture, the schools would have to learn the lower-class social influences and the resulting motivational structures; second, that lower-class motivational structures are learned and reinforced by the social milieu; therefore, it is meaningless to judge behaviors of lower-class children as being abnormal since they are only so when viewed by ethnic, middle-class standards.

It is necessary to understand that Davis is not criticizing middle-class behavior, as this, too, has been learned and reinforced. Instead, he is pointing out that for any communication and learning to take place, there must be an understanding of the genesis of the behavior and motivations exhibited by the children.

McCandless (1967) has also studied social forces at work in the classroom. In his chapter, "The Middle Class Teacher and the Every Class Child," McCandless has looked at different sets of values and attitudes brought to the classroom by children of a variety of social backgrounds and contrasts these attitudes and values with those of the typically middle-class teacher. With extreme sensitivity and understanding McCandless not only looks at the differences presented by these opposite groups, but he also attempts to understand what these differences mean to different individuals in the way in which they function within the classroom.

McCandless is one of the few author-researchers to recognize the needs of the teachers in his investigations. He recognized these needs particularly as they relate to the types of satisfactions the teacher gains from interacting with the children in the classroom and the way these interactions affect the teacher's responses to children. He observes that children from lower socioeconomic classes are, on the whole, less clean, more overtly aggressive, more overtly sexual (even in the elementary grades), less concerned with clean and correct speech, more overtly hostile, and in general offering less satisfaction and less hope for satisfaction of profiting from the activities of the classroom. It is small wonder, he reasons, that the teacher's attention is directed more to the student who shares values similar to those of the teacher, and in whom the teacher finds greater reward for her efforts with the class.

McCandless looks at the classroom situation through the eyes of the child as well. Particularly in the eyes of the child from the lower socioeconomic class, the teacher may be seen as a hostile stranger making unusual and unreasonable demands. McCandless raises the question of why the child should feel obliged to conform to the demands of the classroom, particularly when the types of behavior and responses which are desired in many instances are contrary to the types of values which are reinforced and rewarded in his own milieu.

Examining the issue further, McCandless states that only to the extent the child from the "other culture" sees the possibility of acceptance into the majority group (i.e., the middle-class group) will he conform to the expected behavior of the group and of the teacher. If, as is often the case, the child sees little or no chance of acceptance by the group, he is unlikely to conform to the behavior of the group.

In brief, what McCandless demonstrates is that the ability of the child is only one factor on which we should concentrate when we are concerned with the development of the child, and in turn relating his development to our process of evaluating the child. His development is as much a function of the values and atti-

116

tudes the child brings with him to the class, which he has learned from the culture in which he lives, as it is of his actual intellectual ability. In addition, the real hope of the child's accepting the standards of the class lies in part with his perception of his chances of being accepted in the majority group.

In looking at studies such as these we must keep in mind that the groups of people we are dealing with are not homogenous. Any time we speak of groups we have built in some type of arbitrary parameters in order to define the group. Thus, when we speak of what a group does or thinks, we are merely stating what *typically* the group does or thinks. There is variability within any group we may thus set up. While we might talk about first graders or second graders as a group, no first or second grade teacher would need to be convinced of the variability of behavior within the group. The same is also true of any group we mention; variability in attitudes and behavior will always be found in these groups.

Other research has also been undertaken relating to the factors which influence personal and academic development. Combs (1968) has suggested that we tend to underestimate the extent of human abilities and likewise tend to concentrate on

117

the limitations rather than the possibilities of human endeavor. Part of the reason for our emphasis of limitations, he maintains, stems from our comparison of intellectual abilities with the medical model or the physical capacities of man. Even here, however, the comparison has been incomplete because we have not fully considered physical capacities in their total range. As an example, Combs cites those stressful emergency situations, of which we have all read, where the individual is called upon to perform physical tasks beyond the expected range of ability. We would not, for example, normally expect a ten-year-old boy to lift two-hundred pounds or a frail one-hundred-pound mother of a teenager to lift an automobile. Yet, these and countless other extraordinary feats have been accomplished in stressful situations. A ten-year-old boy has been reported carrying a two-hundred-pound aquarium from a burning house because the fish were his pets. A one-hundred-pound mother has been reported lifting an automobile which had slipped from a jack in order to free her teenage son pinned under the automobile. Combs feels that given optimal circumstances the individual is capable of performing mental tasks far beyond what one might normally expect.

Combs feels that we are especially likely to underestimate the learning ability of students because of two factors: 1) our failure to admit the whole individual to the classroom and 2) some notions we have concerning failure.

The need to admit the whole individual to the classroom. Combs suggests that we reexamine a long standing notion of the separation of the knowing-learning self and the feeling self of the individual. That is, we have failed to recognize any relationship between the affective (feeling or emotional) side of the individual and the cognitive (knowing-learning) side of the individual. Indeed, Combs suggests that in many situations it is almost as if we ask the individual to leave the affective part of the self outside the classroom because we are only concerned with instructing the cognitive part of the individual.

He cites as an example of the separation described above, the situation in an elementary classroom where, near the end of the day, the topic of love came up. Because the teacher was tired, she allowed the children to discuss love. Later, having some feelings of guilt because the children were not discussing academic matters, she decided to base an assignment on the discussion and asked the children to write a

119

letter telling her of the class discussion. When she read the children's letters she was struck by the amazement of the children that a topic such as love could be discussed in class.

While there are many aspects of this issue which could be discussed, there are two areas of particular importance which deserve further consideration. The first is best exemplified by a further illustration which Combs uses. He tells of an elementary class on a field trip to the art museum. Just inside the entranceway to the museum was a huge painting. A group of children upon entering the museum were awed by the size of the painting and stood gazing at it, their mouths agape in amazement. The teacher in rounding up the children urged the group along by saying, "If you children don't hurry up you are not going to get to see anything!" The point Combs is making in this anecdote is that in American education particularly, we tend to confuse quantity with quality. In another article (1966) he maintains that one of the problems of education is that children fail to learn not because they were not told, but because they were never helped in understanding what the learning meant to them. The problem, according to Combs, is not a failure to provide students with facts, but rather a need to help the students integrate these facts into their own personal lives.

A final consideration concerning admitting the whole child to the classroom is related to Combs' examination of the concept the individual has of himself (1972). This area of concern has also been studied with adults where an attempt was made to determine how the individual's view of himself is related to his success in his given occupation. A wide range of occupations was represented in the study including nurses, teachers, priests, etc. There were clear indications that those who felt they were competent in their chosen field were judged by their peers to be in fact competent. The converse of this was also true, i.e., those who did not feel competent in their chosen field were not judged as being competent by others.

In school as well, the child who feels he is capable of doing the task at hand most often is the one who does achieve in that given area. Likewise, the child who for any reason feels he cannot achieve a given task is most likely to be the one who will not achieve in that area.

Research has also been undertaken with young children, studying the child's self-concept as it relates to various types of achievement. Coopersmith (1967) has reported the results of eight years of study,

121

which is still in progress. His results tend to confirm Combs' findings. Purkey (1970), who has examined the area of self-concept and achievement, characterizes both the successful and unsuccessful student. Of the successful student he states:

> The conclusion that the successful student is one who is likely to see himself in essentially positive ways has been verified by a host of studies. . . .
>
> A composite portrait of the successful student would seem to show that he has a relatively high opinion of himself and is optimistic about his future performance. (Ringness, 1961) He has confidence in his general ability (Taylor, 1964) and in his ability as a student. (Brookover, 1969) He needs further favorable evaluations from others (Dittes, 1959), and he feels that he works hard, is liked by other students, and is generally polite and honest. (Davidson and Greenberg, 1967) Judging by their statements, successful students can generally be characterized as having positive self-concepts and tending to excel in feelings of worth as individuals. (pp. 18–20)

Purky also characterizes the unsuccessful student as follows:

They tend to see themselves as less able, less adequate, and less self-reliant than their more successful peers. This is particularly true of boys, and it is also true, but to a lesser extent, of girls. Students with negative self-images of ability rarely perform well in school, as the research of Brookover, Erickson, and Joiner (1967) has indicated. Of even more sinister significance, continued feelings of worthlessness are, as Fromm (1941, 1947) points out, characteristic of the unhealthy personality. The basic question of whether children see themselves negatively because of their poor school performance, or whether they perform poorly in school because they see themselves negatively, is unresolved. (pp. 22–23)

Some notions we have concerning failure. Combs' second point, which is pertinent to our emphasis on the limitations of the individual, is concerned with some conceptions, or perhaps misconceptions, of failure. He suggests that there is a prevailing notion that failure is good for the individual, and that we learn from failure. Often, he states, it is the self-made man who makes pronouncements on the benefits of failure, citing his prior failure

123

as the reason for his success. Combs contends that the self-made man is a glaring contradiction of his own argument, for he is a success, not as a result of his failures but as a result of his successes.

He makes a convincing analogy of exposure to failure in school to medical inoculation against a serious disease. We do not expose the child directly to the disease since the results could be fatal. Instead, we expose the child to the disease in an attenuated form so that the child is successfully able to resist the disease. Combs suggests that academic failure, too, should be presented in an attenuated form so that the child can learn to successfully cope with it.

Certainly no discussion of child behavior, in virtually any area of expression, could be undertaken without consideration of the writings and comments of Jerome Kagan. While there are a host of areas about which Kagan has written, there are two areas which are of particular importance to a survey of evaluation concerns: 1) sex differences and 2) motivation.

Sex differences. Kagan in his considerations of this topic (1956, 1961, 1964, 1969) has viewed the topic from a number of different perspectives. One of the key issues which has touched off research is the generally accepted notion that disciplinary problems and retardation in both reading and over-all academic achievement are five times more prevalent in boys than girls in the early elementary grades. One of the popular explanations of this phenomenon has been that girls are on the average approximately six months more mature than boys at this age.

While Kagan accepts this as a partial explanation, he suggests that other factors are at work as well. One of these factors with which he has been particularly concerned is that of sex role identification. About the time that boys typically enter school, and for approximately the next two to three years, they are busily engaged in identifying with appropriate sex role behavior. That is, the young boy observes adult male models and attempts to emulate them by undertaking activities which are appropriate to the sex role.

In this process the typical boy observes that his father is the dominant figure in the household, and part of this dominant stature deemphasizes the adult female role. As a result, the young boy entering school appears to be less anxious to please the female teacher than his female counterpart, who in her own sex role identification would typically be currying the favor of the adult in general, and the adult female in particular.

A second facet of this phenomenon is that the child has learned that the gender of an activity or object, if one can label such a phenomenon, is determined by the gender of the individual who typically participates in or monitors the activity. This process apparently does not depend upon external logic, but rather it fulfills the requirements stated above. Thus, skipping rope, which most would concede to be a very strenuous activity, would typically be labeled by boys as being feminine, because girls do it. An exception might be found in the boy whose father is an athlete (e.g., a boxer). Then the activity would be viewed as being masculine since the primary source of sex role identification is engaged in this activity.

Kagan (1964) suggests this identification of activities carries over into the school setting. In most instances the child's first contact with school is under the supervision of a female teacher. Because of this, the boy typically views the school setting as being feminine in orientation, and he is therefore less anxious to conform and achieve than are girls.

Kagan (1969) notes a general exception to the theory he has postulated when he observes that boys whose fathers work with books, pencils, and other school related materials have more of a masculine orientation to school, in the same way that the example cited above was altered in the boxer's son's view of skipping rope.

While Kagan's studies have received a great deal of attention, there are some conflicting results coming out of research related to this problem. Studies reported by Strickler and Phillips (1970) and Dolan (1969) have given informal support to the notion of a male teacher at the kindergarten level. By "informal" it is meant there was no rigorous examination of differences between sex-segregated kindergartens and the typical coed kindergarten. Enthusiasm, however, was reported from both students and parents in the sex-segregated kindergarten, and Dolan does report a very low rate of absenteeism on the part of boys in his "stag" kindergarten as compared with the typical attendance rate at this grade level for boys.

Curtis (1968) reports that where it normally takes boys about half of the school year to get ready for reading, in an all male first grade the boys were ready for reading by the second month.

Bolig (1971), in more rigorous research and using a modification of sex-segregated kindergarten, has been able to demonstrate only partial support of the theory.

In his study, Bolig's kindergarten settings were sex-segregated, but were taught by female teachers. In the all male kindergartens the activities, materials, and equipment were geared to boys' interests. After random placement and initial testing Bolig retested at the end of the school year and found:

Academic readiness, as measured by the Metropolitan Readiness Test, was significantly greater for children in the sex-segregated classes: the girls profited most, and the boys profited more than either girls or boys in integrated classes. (p. 71)

Bolig's findings, however, did not confirm Kagan's findings, in that both boys' and girls' perceptions of school, in both the integrated and sex-segregated classes, remained unchanged throughout the course of the experiment.

This area of study, as one would anticipate, has, in turn, stimulated research in related areas. Pollack (1968) has raised the question of teacher bias against boys, particularly as it relates to evaluation, and Sexton (1970) raised a number of questions concerning the ways the school system feminizes boys. Sexton's questions and criticisms are extensions of much of what has previously been discussed. Miss Sexton is concerned with the high number of women teachers in the elementary school (eighty-five percent) and the number of women teachers K–12 (sixty-eight percent). Her concern primarily lies with the pervasive influence of women teachers in setting the standards both academically and in terms of standards of behavior. She feels that most boys who attempt to succeed in an institution dominated by women tend to become feminized in the process. She argues that a person's life-style should be individually chosen, and that under the current female influence of the schools it is more difficult for the boy to assert his masculinity—or the girl who wishes to assert herself—to do so and succeed in the institution.

Sexton's suggestion for resolution of the problem is not to do away with the schools, but rather, to attempt to find some redirection which will permit a broader set of responses than we typically find.

One response to these issues has been the recognized need for different types of curricular materials. While materials are being developed in a number of quarters, *The Checkered Flag Series* (Bamman and

Whitehead, 1968) is one such example. It is of interest to note the following statements in the "Introduction" to the teacher's manual.

> Boys constitute nine-tenths of the reading problem cases in our schools. Certainly the slower development of boys at early stages, cultural expectations which fail to encourage boys to become good readers, and a lack of appropriate materials which truly awaken interests in boys are reasons for some of the failures. The interests of boys and girls diverge during early school years; still, little effort has been made to provide in basic materials, ideas, and situations which relate to the interests of boys alone, or of girls alone. . . . *The Checkered Flag Series* has been written for boys, with the firm conviction that girls will be interested in these stories too. While there are no major feminine characters in the stories, strong characterizations of both boys and men carry universal appeal. (1968, pp. 1–2.)

Some have obviously taken objection to masculinized materials essentially on the grounds we will merely reverse the situation by correcting the problem for boys and creating a new problem for girls.

Kagan (1969) has taken the position that through cultural conditioning, girls are adult pleasers as children, and they would therefore remain unaffected by masculinized curriculum. Additionally, there is still the female teacher who would hopefully offset any negative aspects of a masculinized curriculum.

Another solution to this potential problem is to have a twofold curriculum for the sexes in the early elementary grades. Some would advocate separate classrooms, one for males and one for females, in the early elementary years. This, of course, has been tried in experimental situations with mixed results, as reported earlier.

While the number of observations have been limited, it has been my observation where masculinized reading materials were being used the girls soon grew tired of them as "dumb old boys' stories" and soon sought out literature on their own that was more to their liking.

Two other aspects of sex differences in the early grades are worth noting. One stems from the research of physiologists who have noted that boys typically have a larger muscle mass than girls even at the early elementary age. As a result, it is physiologically more difficult for boys to remain seated, quiet, and in an attentive posture for long periods of time. While this is often interpreted by elementary teachers as evidence that boys are more immature than girls or are less interested in what goes on in the classroom, the fact is there is a physiological explanation for their behavior. Boys need the opportunity for periodic respites from sitting, and particularly the opportunity to engage in activities which require the use of the large muscles.

Recently, research has also pointed out that boys are more prone to hyperkinetic activity or what is more commonly referred to as the "Jumping Jack Syndrome." These are the children who are almost constantly in motion either by jumping out of their seats and wandering around or, who even when standing, rock back and forth constantly. This is a form of unusual behavior which is essentially beyond the scope of this book, and the presentation here is no attempt at a careful diagnostic description. It is of concern to us, however, in that the "Jumping Jack Syndrome" is estimated to affect as many as 3,000,000 children under the age of fifteen, and estimates are that as many as seventy percent of those afflicted are boys! While the medical treatment of this disorder is beyond the facilities of the typical school, and the child suffering from it needs expert diagnosis and medication, the point being made is that the child's behavior can easily be misunderstood to indicate that he is just not interested in what is going on in class, when in reality he has a medical problem over which the child has no control.

Study in this area of sex differences continues and shows promise of shedding additional light on an area where modifications can be implemented to cope with some of the problems. It gives every indication of being an area of research which will deserve our continued attention and awareness.

Motivation. The area of motivation is extremely complex. There are a number of variables, which will affect an individual's motivational patterns in any type of behavior, such as age, sex, prior experiences, socioeconomic class, etc. Even at the risk of oversimplifying the issue, some remarks may be in order.

Kagan (1969) reports that signs of anxiety concerning the failure of a task are displayed by children as early as eighteen months of age. That is, the child working with a puzzle, for example, may walk away from it, throw the puzzle down, or refuse to even attempt to work with the puzzle when he fails to solve the problem of the puzzle. Of course, there are variations in behavior, as we have noted before, but the point is the anxiety of failure does demonstrate itself at this early age.

So it is, as well, with the school-age child. The strength of his motivation, in the main, is determined by his perception of his ability to resolve the task at hand. Kagan suggests that when the child's perception of success with the task, particularly when the success or failure is public, will determine his reaction. In essence, the child fears failure. This anxiety is so strong in many children that they would rather avoid trying the task than risking failure!

The reverse of this is oddly true as well. That is, the child who is quite confident that he or she can achieve the task will typically have minimal motivation for success. The optimal conditions for motivation appear to be when the child is not quite sure of his ability to perform the task. He should have reasonable confidence in his abilities but should see the task as, perhaps, a bit beyond him.

The influence of the peer group is likewise a determining factor in the area of motivation and achievement. Rather typically the peer group encourages academic mediocrity. To the extent then that the peer group influences the individual, he may withhold his academic prowess in the classroom.

It must be recognized the converse of this may also be true. That is, the peer group may be in academic competition not only with one another, but also with the rest of the class as well. When this situation exists, assuming the peer group has influence over the individual, he will exert maximal effort to excel to the extent of his capacities in order to effectively compete.

There are an infinite variety of variables which influence and determine the level of motivation. These are but a few examples of the factors interacting with the elementary school age child.

SUMMARY

We have attempted to view some of the factors involved in the process of evaluation in the classroom. They are varied and complex in their nature, and no claim is made that those presented here are complete. What is suggested throughout the chapter, however, is that in the process of evaluation there are a number of rather subtle variables interacting. Many of these variables are so subtle they are not easily recognizable to the teacher, the parent, or even the child. One of the notions which should surface in this chapter is that we should hesitate to label a student as lazy, an overachiever, or not working up to his capacity and should instead be encouraged to look beyond the surface behavior of the child.

In addition, it has strongly been suggested that some of the practices of evaluation also need additional consideration beyond what normally takes place in the classroom. Many of the issues raised here provoke the nagging and knotty questions of "education for what?" and "how will we evaluate it?"

The issues of evaluation have had a number of forums in speeches, debates, professional literature, and informal discussions. These discussions often appear distant and remote, when in reality they take on meaning only at the local level. Ultimately the question of evaluating must rest with the local school and more particularly with the individual classroom teacher, as it is here that choices must be made.

4

Teaching and guidance

INTRODUCTION

Unfortunately, teaching and guidance are often presented as separate entities with the only common ground they share being they both take place within the school and both are concerned with the children in the school. This division is an unfortunate one in that both guidance and teaching should be striving for the achievement of the same goals—the fullest development of the child so that he may live a richer and fuller life.

It has been stated earlier that even when the school has the services of a counselor the focus of guidance is not shifted away from the classroom. This is a firm conviction of many of those who are most deeply committed to the cause of elementary guidance.

Thus far we have looked at some of the practices which teachers normally perform. The primary purpose of the preceding has been to raise questions as to how those practices might be more effectively accomplished.

There are, however, other areas with which we should also be concerned if we wish to help bring about the full development of the child. Those areas which will be considered in this chapter include: 1) the teaching of human relations, 2) career development in the elementary school, and 3) some concluding considerations.

THE TEACHING OF HUMAN RELATIONS

Nearly all who are in education are concerned not only with the child's mastery of academic content, but also with the child's social-interpersonal relationships with his peers and adults. It is distressing to see a child, through his own inappropriate behavior, systematically erect a wall between himself and his peers. It is equally distressing when, for what appears to be no reason, a child is made the scapegoat of the group, and is teased and tormented almost beyond endurance. Education which neglects the social-personal development of the individual is a partial education at best.

We have a vague notion that social behavior is learned, and the approach we use in most adult-child relationships when we wish to alter behavior is lecturing the child or telling him the behavior is inappropriate. Whether we are parent or teacher, we normally find that lecturing is no solution to the problem; it merely gives us a vague awareness that we have recognized the problem and have tried to deal with it. When a parent is summoned to the school to be informed of the child's misbehavior the parent often becomes uneasy and perhaps defensive, and makes a comment similar to, "I don't understand why Johnny acts this way. I've told him time and time again this behavior will get him into difficulty, but he just doesn't listen to me."

We might have greater success in altering the child's behavior if we did something more than tell the child the behavior is inappropriate. If it can be accepted that social relations are learned, even as a child learns his multiplication tables, then perhaps it can also be accepted that, as in the academic setting, merely telling the child a fact does not assure that he will learn it.

Take for example the multiplication tables. No experienced teacher would anticipate that the children would learn merely by being passively instructed. The effective teacher will see that there is involvement on the part of the child to better assure that learning will take place. To this end, the teacher has the child engaged in practice exercises in his seat and at the board; she may divide the room into teams for purposes of group competition or devise a host of other exercises to involve the student in the learning process. She will make certain that involvement on the part of the child in the learning process is active, not trust that once the child is told, with no follow-up activity, he will inevitably learn.

Continuing the analogy, it would be most unusual to anticipate that the child, having one exposure to multiplication tables, even with involvement, will master the subject. We generally recognize that additional consideration and practice are needed in order to develop skills to the point where they are readily available for use.

And, finally, if we are consistent with what has been stated before, we attempt to show the student how the information will be of value to him. That is, we try to help the student understand that this is not an isolated exercise, but that it will be a tool which will be of practical assistance to him in his further education and development. When the learning has practicality and personal meaning, then there is a motive for learning which stimulates the entire process.

The analogy between the learning of academic tasks and of personal behavior could be continued to include other factors such as the futility of corporal punishment when the child fails to learn an academic task. The point of the analogy, however, is that human behavior, whether it is academic, such as learning multiplication tables, or personal, such as learning to interact effectively with one's peers, is learned behavior. Both kinds of behavior are subject to the same laws of learning whether we recognize and understand those laws or not. Personal-social behavior is just as amenable to a planned program of learning as are any of the academic skills.

The analogy, as is often the case, can be overdrawn and oversimplified. Human behavior is complex whether it deals with academic subject matter or personal-social behavior. The example of learning the multiplication tables is inadequate in this sense, in that it is essentially dealing with rote memorization as opposed to the higher levels of reasoning found in abstract analysis. For instance, while the child may learn his multiplication tables with ease, he may have difficulty with the next level of application. He may, for example, be faced with a story problem which involves a series of numbers and with the dilemma of whether he should add, subtract, multiply, or divide. In terms of rote memorization, he may be able to perform any of these skills when they are so designated, but when they are presented in a story problem situation, his problem is not *how* he can apply these skills, but *which* skill he should apply. This requires an understanding at another level.

His problem takes on greater complexity when he moves from the well-defined and precise area of mathematics and becomes involved in other areas of study where answers are less clearly established. If, for example, the child is asked to discuss the significant factors leading to the American Revolution, he must decide for himself which factors are significant. The child may have learned some of the catch phrases such as "taxation without representation is tyranny," "the struggle for independence from the British Crown," and be able to repeat them; but if they have been fed to the child without his really understanding the meaning, he will be unable to discuss them intelligently.

Even here, our analogy may continue to serve us. Attempts to alter human behavior by catch phrases such as, "nice boys don't do that" or "good children will listen to the teacher," without any further explanation or consideration of the child are not only inadequate as efforts for altering behavior, but they may also rob the child of a chance for further development through his own reasoning and understanding of the situation. Clark Moustakas, the eminent child psychotherapist, deals with this notion of teaching by platitude when he stated:

> He (the child) must be respected as he is, with his own concepts and perceptions, however wrong they may be.

> When the teacher forces the child to accept a viewpoint or cuts the child off or pressures him into agreement, the child soon realizes that the only acceptable path is the path of conformity and acceptance of authority. Such a child may become insensitive to himself,

unresponsive to his own experience, and unfeeling in his associations with others. (1961, p. 54)

This use of force on the part of the teacher may be of the gentle persuasion variety, as in this hypothetical conversation between a teacher and a child:

Teacher: You know that nice boys don't do that, don't you?

Child: Yes.

Teacher: And you want to be a nice boy don't you?

The child really has no choice in the answer he must give the teacher.

Several points have been made here which need to be viewed in the perspective of personal-social behavior.

1. Human behavior is learned behavior. This is true not only of academic types of behavior, but personal-social behavior as well.

2. Human behavior is guided by general learning principles. This is true whether we are aware of these principles or not. Our lack of familiarity with or understanding of learning principles in no way suspends these principles. One of our tasks as educators is to be constantly striving to both understand and employ these principles in promoting maximum

development of the children and youth with whom we work.

3. Very basically some learning principles which are common to both academic learning and personal-social learning include an interaction among the factors of receiving information, involvement with the learning process, and a repetition in learning and using newly acquired skills. The principle of involvement is based on the premise that the child must see both the problem and the information within the context of his own range of experiences so that dealing with the problem has purpose, meaning, and practicality for him. The principle of repetition is based on the observation that when the child has been behaving inappropriately, no matter how effective the adult assistance may be in guiding the child toward more positive behavior, new behavior will not be adopted immediately. As in the learning of any new skill, there must be some opportunity to develop and polish an appropriate repertoire. It cannot be overemphasized that the teacher must not become discouraged at her inability to effect change in the behavior of the child the first time she tries, any more than she would anticipate altering his behavior on the first attempt with an academic skill.

The question may legitimately be

raised, "What can I do in the classroom to promote the development of more effective human relationships?" There are a number of possible exercises which can be employed in the typical classroom. Some will be discussed in the following sections.

Unfinished stories

One method which can be employed to promote development in human relations can be classified under the general heading of the unfinished story. It has been used over the years with a wide range of age groups, and when effectively presented it has tended to develop an understanding of others and to promote personal-social skills.

The basic procedure is to present a story which is appropriate to the age group and involves a dramatic incident leading to a problem that calls for a solution. When the problem is presented the story breaks off, usually with the question of what the person or persons involved should do. There is no right or wrong answer for the persons involved in this type of situation, but instead, there are a number of effective ways the individuals in the story might proceed in order to solve the problem.

There are a number of developmental characteristics which may evolve through the use of the unfinished story. First, all who participate in this type of activity may begin to see the relationship between cause and effect in human relationships. That is, they may realize, often for the first time, that the circumstances of a given situation or the ways people respond to an individual in the situation determine how the individual will respond to those who are interacting with him. Adults may think it obvious that there is a cause for an individual's behavior, but this is not always true with children. While children may be somewhat cognizant of the fact that they respond in different ways to different people, typically the child does not analyze the situation. As a result, children may often resort to generalizations about other children with such comments as, "Oh, that is just Fred. He always acts that way." While the comment may be true in that Fred does always act that way, it is an oversimplification to write off his behavior as being just that and nothing more. We tend to think that descriptive statements about an individual explain his behavior, which of course is not true. The more penetrating question might be, "What is there in my behavior or the behavior of others which causes Fred to respond the way he does?"

Oddly enough gains in understanding

of cause and effect in human relationships are not confined entirely to children. Even teachers who already give every indication of being sensitive to the children they teach have indicated that using the process of the unfinished story has reawakened an understanding of human behavior, which through the normal course of activity perhaps had become somewhat dulled.

Once the children have developed an understanding of this process it is amazing to note how far the learning manifests itself. One brief example may be appropriate. Some years ago when I was affiliated with a public school, the physical plant of the school was designed in a series of separate buildings comprising a campus type of school. At one end of the cluster of buildings were classes for the mentally retarded and emotionally disturbed. One day while walking between buildings, I came upon a veteran second grader who had been exposed to a program in understanding human behavior showing a new second grader where the various buildings in the complex were located. The new student suddenly asked his guide, "Show me the building where the dumb crazy kids are." With firmness and yet politeness the guide stated, "At this school we don't call children those names. If you want to go to the building where they teach the mentally retarded and emotionally disturbed children I will be glad to show it to you." From the look on the newcomer's face, it is doubtful that he ever referred to the "dumb crazy kids" again.

The second advantage of the unfinished story approach to human development is contained in the process itself. Through this approach the children are dealing with situations that are familiar to them in terms of content and problems. The children have the opportunity to stand back, so to speak, and to objectively look at situations they themselves might well be involved in. Through this objectivity they are able to examine the issues involved and attempt to propose a variety of ways in which the characters in the story might act to bring about an effective resolution to the problem.

This approach is a natural for children. Anyone who has watched a child engrossed in a play, a television story, a story read aloud, or a puppet show knows the ease with which a child becomes involved in a story line.

Myers (1970) employed a similar technique using puppets in working with retarded children in a state hospital setting. With appropriate experimental controls for his study, he found that children who were involved in puppetry where children worked out the solution to the conflict showed significant positive changes in their social behavior on the wards of the hospital. Equally significant, he also found that even relatively untrained personnel were able to conduct puppetry sessions with effective results.

The availability of materials for the unfinished story presents no problem. Stories for use in the classroom situation are available from a number of sources. Perhaps the most readily available and most widely used is from the National Education Association. Since 1961 the N.E.A. has published unfinished stories in the *N.E.A. Journal*. These unfinished stories have been accumulated into two separate publications that include the most popular stories. These publications are available for a nominal charge from the National Education Association. (Order from N.E.A. Publication Sales Section, 1201 16th Street, N.W., Washington, D.C. 20036. Request *Unfinished Stories for Use in the Classroom* or *More Unfinished Stories for Use in the Classroom.*)

In order for the reader to better understand the nature of the unfinished story, one example from *Unfinished Stories for Use in the Classroom* is presented.

What should Henry do?

The old ramshackle barn at the end of the alley behind the school had everything you could imagine in it—a Model T Ford, a bear trap, and, according to some people, even a coffin in the loft.

Imagining was all the school kids could do, though. The owner, Mr. McGowan, had posted a No Trespassing sign on it, and the school had a rule that any pupil who even went into the alley during recess or lunch time would be barred from school clubs and other activities for the rest of the year.

Henry was captain of the kickball team and belonged to the stamp club. He certainly didn't want to give up those activities, but he kept remembering the wonderful tales he'd heard about the barn. Was there really a coffin in the loft? Was it an empty coffin?

One misty day during lunch period, Henry's curiosity got the better of him. He'd heard that Mr. McGowan had sprained his ankle, and decided that now, if ever, was his chance to explore the barn.

He slipped out of the school yard when none of his friends were looking and darted down the alley to the big barn. Somewhere on its weather-beaten roof, a shingle flapped in the wind. Henry pulled the great creaking door open and slipped inside. He couldn't see very well in the darkness, but thought he could see the ladder leading to the loft. He started to make his way over to it.

Henry had taken two or three steps when he heard a soft, groaning noise. Terrified, he stood stock-still for a moment. The groaning continued. Could it be coming from the coffin?

"I'm going to get out of here," Henry said to himself, turning toward the door. Then he stopped as he heard the noise again. Now he felt sure that those groans were coming from someone or something alive, someone or something in pain or in trouble.

Henry hesitated. Should he track down the groans himself or should he go for help? What if the groans were coming from some sick or injured animal, vicious with pain? And if the groans were human groans, what could he do to help?

Henry pushed his way through the door and started to run to the McGowan house. A thought caught him up short. He would have to tell Mr. McGowan that he had been in the barn. No matter what happened, grouchy old Mr. Mc-Gowan would be bound to tell the principal that Henry had broken the rule about the barn, and that would be the end of kickball and stamp club for Henry.

Why tell anybody? Henry asked himself. If he hadn't gone into the barn, he wouldn't have heard the groaning. He wasn't really *supposed* to hear it. Maybe what he'd heard was only the wind, anyhow. Why should he give up kickball and stamp club just because somebody or something might need help? But he kept remembering those awful groans. What should Henry do?

Possible discussion topics:

1. What reasons might Mr. McGowan have for not wanting the boys in the barn?
2. What might have been making the noises Henry heard?
3. Should Henry risk getting in trouble himself by trying to help when he is not sure anything is wrong?
4. If Henry knew that a sick person or animal was making the noises, should he tell someone and risk being punished for being in the barn?

·(1966, p. 16)

In addition to the N.E.A. series there are other stories available from a variety of sources which are easily used in the classroom by the teacher. Sound filmstrips such as Guidance Associates' "First Things" series which employ the same principle as the unfinished stories can also be effectively used. Still another source, which is focused from the individual's point of view in self-discovery, is found in *Dimensions of Personality* series. (Limbacher, 1969, 1970) Where there is some assistance from a school psychologist or school social worker there is yet another series which is quite effective for classroom use which is similar in format to the N.E.A. series, *A Teaching Program In Human Behavior and Mental Health.* (Ojemann, 1964) Additionally, the resourceful teacher can make up stories and materials of her own for classroom use.

Use of the unfinished story in the classroom

The ways in which unfinished stories can be used in the classroom are limited only by the teacher's imagination. For maximal use of these materials, two general guidelines deserve our consideration.

1. For developing personal-social skills, this use of the stories should be part of a developmental process. That is, the program should be a continuous one from

kindergarten through the fifth or sixth grade, depending upon the structure of the school. Obviously, the stories used would have to be appropriate to the group in terms of age and experiences. Some experimentation will be necessary to find stories which capture the students' attention and involvement. As is true in any exercise within the classroom, stories which are popular and have a high degree of involvement one year may generate little or no interest the following year.

2. The unfinished story approach can readily be included as part of the curriculum. Unfinished stories are particularly a natural part of English, language development, or social studies courses. By not being a "regular feature" of the curriculum, the unfinished stories retain their spontaneity and interest appeal for students, so that the students are eager to participate and do not come to regard this activity as merely routine, as sometimes happens with regular classroom activities.

Among the almost limitless approaches to the use of the unfinished story, here is an example of one teacher's approach.

An unfinished story was read to an entire class of thirty-five students. Immediately after the reading of the story, the students were asked to write their reaction to the dilemma presented in the story and to state what they would do if they faced the same problem. The next day the group was divided into three small groups where the children had the opportunity to discuss the situation involved in the story. During this time in the small group there was a free flow of ideas among the children as to what had happened and what might be done to resolve the situation. After a twenty-minute discussion in the small groups the children were asked to write a second personal reaction to the situation and again were asked to state what they would do. The following day, the teacher once again read the story to the entire class and invited the class to discuss the story. Again, after twenty minutes to a half an hour of discussion, the teacher asked each of the students to write an individual reaction to the situation as well as write what he would do. (The author appreciates the cooperation of Miss Marena Basos, a former elementary teacher in the Bethlehem, Hanover Elementary School, for permission to report on this classroom activity.)

This particular approach was helpful in a number of ways. It permitted the teacher to introduce the concept of unfinished stories to the class in a way which stimulated discussion through small

156

group participation at the outset. In addition, through the two group exposures, it permitted the teacher to see the group interaction and its effect on the attitudes of children. And, finally, it gave the teacher the opportunity to see the development of attitudes, and in some instances attitude change, through the individual papers which the children had written. Through this process the teacher was able to observe an increase of flexibility in the child's responses, a growing tolerance toward others' behavior, and a more constructive attitude in resolving the problem presented.

Perhaps the single most important practice the teacher must keep in mind in working with unfinished stories is to avoid imposing her point of view into the discussion, and to prevent any individual or individuals from either monopolizing discussion or exerting undue influence in expressing their opinions. The importance of avoiding such influence cannot be stressed too strongly. In addition, it is important that the children understand that there is no right or wrong answer, but rather that they are looking for a variety of solutions, some of which may be more effective than others.

When properly used, the unfinished story can be quite similar to a simulation

157

exercise which can be effective in promoting the growth and development in an area which is often overlooked or taken for granted.

Life space interviews

Inevitably in the classroom setting, as well as in all other facets of human interaction, conflicts will emerge between children and occasionally between child and teacher. The more common occurrence, of course, is overt conflict between children.

The typical adult approach to these strained relationships between children, whether he be teacher, parent, or any other adult, is a question, "All right, who started this?" Another approach frequently used is, "This is no way to settle differences. Now, let's shake hands and be friends."

These two approaches are superficial at best. The first seems to be based on the adult conception of legal rights, which typically has little meaning to the child. Obviously both children thought they were right, or that they had been wronged, or the difficulty would not have occurred at the outset.

The second approach is expedient and nothing more. It implies that the situation is disruptive, but that superficial conformity to the code of behavior of the classroom is more important than a resolution of the conflict or a consideration of feelings of the children involved.

Life space interviewing, conflict counseling, and a variety of other names have been applied to an approach which suggests that the dynamics of the interaction which has taken place is of the greatest importance. Life space interviewing is the process of dealing directly with the issues involved in a conflict between individuals in such a manner that those involved gain a recognition and understanding of the circumstances involved. The basic notion, of course, is to help individuals understand what happened so that they are in a better position to *learn* from the situation. This type of approach does not require that the adult involved be knowledgeable in terms of profound personal dynamics or that she be highly skilled in therapeutic techniques, but that she be alert and sensitive to the interaction of children and capable of helping children to discover why they reacted as they did in a particular situation.

Morse (1963) looks at the life space interview from the viewpoint of the classroom teacher and sees six steps involved in the process. Briefly summarizing Morse's points we note:

1. The teacher should permit the

child to express the problem situation in his own words, and more importantly, from his own point of view. This should be done even though the teacher may feel the child's perception of the situation is distorted.

2. The teacher should attempt to determine if the problem situation is an isolated incident or whether it is related to other forms of behavior of the particular child.

3. The teacher should attempt to elicit from the child how he feels the problem should be dealt with. This involves a number of variables which include seeing how the child is able to incorporate the situation in question into his over-all mode of response, his resistance to being involved in the resolution of the situation, or his over-all resistance to change.

4. The teacher should help the child deal with the reality of the school environment; that is, he should explain the ramifications for the student, should his behavior continue to remain unchanged. This explanation should not be undertaken in a threatening, preachy, or moralistic style, but it should be presented in a calm, objective manner, assisting the child to determine his obligations to the social order in which he operates.

5. At this stage the teacher should discuss with the child how he might deal with the same or similar problems in the future. In addition, the teacher might ask the child how she might reasonably and realistically support him in his particular quest. Morse cautions the reader at this point on the folly of expecting immediate and lasting results from this single discussion.

6. Finally, the teacher should explore with the child the realistic possibilities of courses of action which might result from repetition of similar behavior. Again, this should be presented in an objective manner, and in one which is realistic within the framework of the operation of the school.

Morse suggests this entire process has a twofold purpose: first, gaining an understanding of the child's perception and understanding of the situation; and second, helping the child to understand the realities of the environment in which he operates and to understand how his behavior in that environment will determine future courses of action.

In essence, the approach suggested in the life space interviewing is effective teaching. If an analogy can be used, let us look again to the academic setting. If a child or children failed to learn a given

161

academic task, no effective teacher would make the statement, "In this class we expect you to learn how to do this. Now, say you are sorry for not learning it, and the next time learn it." This approach would be both ineffective and silly. Nor would the effective teacher determine who was "right" in solving an academic task and who was "wrong," and expect all the children to successfully complete the task the "right" way in the future. Instead of using either of the above methods, the effective teacher helps the child understand why he could not solve the task and learn what he needs to know to successfully cope with the task in the future. A conflict situation in the class should be viewed as any other learning situation.

The teacher becomes a facilitator with the children in helping them understand their own behavior, which would include an understanding of the effect of one child's behavior on another child's actions. There is no notion of "right" or "wrong," but rather a learning and understanding of what happened and why it happened. Ideally, a discussion should take place as soon after the conflict as is reasonably possible. It may be advisable to talk with the offended parties individually before bringing the two together.

The critical point involved here is the

increased understanding each child gains as a result of the conflict, and the tremendous opportunity for growth which it provides. Moustakas states this quite well.

> This is exactly what a true confrontation offers—an opportunity for the teacher to meet the child on a new and vital level.
> The confrontation offers the chance for a completely new understanding and awareness because it is not a routine exchange between individuals. It is a real meeting, a coming to grips with life. It is a challenge to all of the teacher's reserve. It brings strength where there is weakness, good where there is evil, openness where there is restrictiveness, beauty where there is ugliness.
> Conflict with a pupil can be the supreme test for the teacher. But the teacher must face this conflict bravely and with love; when he does both he and the child come through the experience to a meaningful way of life, a life where confidence continues unshaken, even strengthened. (1961, p. 54)

The question will inevitably come up, "But where will I find the time? What do I do with the rest of the children?" There can be no universal answer since every

163

school will function in a different manner, as will each teacher. The point is that if attitudes and personal development are as important as we claim they are, we will find time for these functions, just as we create the opportunity to help the child who is encountering academic difficulty. If we feel the task is truly important enough, we will find the time for it.

Sociometry

Another of the approaches which can be used in the classroom to promote human relationships is the use of sociometric instruments which can help the teacher see the positive and negative interactions among the students in the class, from the child's point of view. Sociometric methods, for example, have long been advocated and used to see the entire personal structure of the group which can give a view of the class structure as perceived by the students. Many teachers reject this method on the basis of knowing their class. While this may be true from the teacher's perspective, it is equally important for the teacher to know the class from the children's perspective. The child who is viewed by the teacher as being neat, orderly, and well behaved, which from the teacher's perspective may be quite good, may be rejected by the other children in the class for many of the very reasons the teacher views the child positively.

By use of sociometric devices the teacher gains a child's eye view of his classmates. In addition to gaining another perspective of the children, the teacher may also gain insight into how to work with a given child or children to assist them in interacting more effectively with their peers. For example, as previously noted, the teacher may view a given child in very positive terms and find the child is rejected by the rest of the class. The teacher may find that she is partially responsible for this rejection because of the way she responds to the child and because of special privileges she may have unknowingly granted the child. Sociometric devices also provide the teacher with feedback on the success or the lack of success of any program she may initiate to work with this situation in changing attitudes toward a child or a group of children.

Finally, brief mention should also be made of the use of role playing as a means of helping children to understand the dynamics of interpersonal relationships. Through the use of role playing either real situations occurring in school or hypothetical—but typical—situations children

Role playing

165

encounter can be examined. In this type of activity children assume different roles involved in the situation which they act out in an attempt to find some resolution to the problem at hand. Role playing can be used quite readily with unfinished stories as well, in acting out a solution to the problem presented to the class. In using role playing with the unfinished stories children would assume the roles of the individuals involved in the unfinished story and attempt to present the story as authentically as possible. One of the primary benefits of such an approach is that it gives to children an opportunity to test the reality of some of their recommendations for resolving the situation presented to them. If the children are able to present their roles accurately, they can quickly see the effectiveness or the ineffectiveness of their proposed recommendation.

While research is still somewhat lacking in role playing as it relates to elementary school children, some cautions are suggested, two of which stand out:

1. The group size should not be too large. Normally, five or less children is considered the maximum size in order for all the children to participate fully. (Kranzler et al, 1966; Ohlsen, 1964)

2. If the teacher chooses to assume a role in the role-play situation, she should

play an adult role. Children tend to find it both confusing and inhibiting to view the teacher in a child's role. It presents a problem to the child in a role-play situation to respond to the teacher as a peer. Even if he is able to respond in the role-play situation, it is difficult for the child to transfer back to a student-teacher relationship once the activity is terminated. (Lippman, 1962)

The list of approaches to the teaching of human relationships could continue, but the central notion of all these activities is that the child is presented with a variety of situations which give him the opportunity to explore cause and effect in human interaction. It also provides him a laboratory setting where he can safely try out and practice ideas and methods of human relationships.

CAREER DEVELOPMENT IN THE ELEMENTARY SCHOOL

Career development has played a part in the elementary guidance function since the early part of the 1960s. Almost as soon as it became clear there would be an upsurge in the number of elementary school counselors, various groups began to suggest what the functions of these counselors should be. Among the first to make recommendations were those who were

167

concerned with career development, and their articles appeared in *The Vocational Guidance Quarterly,* presenting a broad spectrum of opinions and recommendations. (Arbuckle, 1964; Grell, 1960; Kaback, 1960; Kaye, 1960; Nelson, 1962; Tennyson, 1964; Barbe and Chambers, 1963)

Theories concerning career choice have been undergoing serious reconsideration. Much of the theory and practice of career choice during the current century had been influenced by Frank Parsons' writings (1908), which viewed career choice essentially as an event in time in terms of matching the person and the job. During the decade of the fifties thinking concerning career choice underwent a change. The most notable aspect of this change was that career choice began to be viewed as a developmental process rather than as a single event which took place at the time the student either terminated his secondary school education or graduated from high school. In brief, the more recent theories concerning career choice recognized that the choice resulted from a long-standing developmental process of the individual which unfolded and developed over the course of years, much as the personality or academic talents develop. In fact, personality development and academic development are very much a part of the whole process of career development. Thus, the writings of such theoreticians and practitioners as Ginzberg, Ginsburg, Axelrad, and Herma (1951), Hoppock (1957), Super (1957), Roe (1956), and Holland (1959) presented a fresh dimension to the area of career development.

The common characteristic of most of these researchers is that they see career choice as an ongoing and changing process which starts with the child's earliest recognitions and probably does not terminate until death. All the significant events in the child's life help shape and influence the type of career choice he makes. Such factors as the child's academic ability, the make-up of his general temperament, his physical stamina, the types of individuals who are important to him, the basic information and understandings he has of various occupations—all of these and a myriad of other factors become influential as the child makes even tentative choices of his future career. The implications for the elementary school are staggering and yet, in some instances, have been misunderstood.

Probably one of the most devastating errors has been to interpret this newer approach to mean that the child should make his final career choice while he is still in the elementary school, so that he can get on the "right track" by the time he enters the middle school or the junior high school, whichever the case may be. One of the grossest misinterpretations that I am aware of was made in a school district where fifth-grade students were administered the Kuder Preference Record, and based on these results the children were advised as to what their career choices should be. Schools encouraging practices such as this have obviously missed the point.

What is actually suggested over-all in these theories is the child's need for a broad exposure to the world of work to assist in his developmental process of making choices based on more complete information, rather than being restricted to taking what is immediately available. One could say that each child lives in his own ghetto, whether it is deprived or affluent, to the extent that his view of the world of work is narrow and restricted. His horizons need to be broadened essentially for several basic reasons:

1. He needs to appreciate the dignity of work. This goes beyond the so-called Protestant Ethic that hard work has its own virtue. What is involved is an understanding and appreciation of the individual who does the work. In our society,

and in nearly all societies, we tend to somehow evaluate the individual by the job he performs. We need to reawaken in ourselves, perhaps, and in the children with whom we work, the value and dignity of both the individual and the work he performs.

2. The child also needs to appreciate the interdependence in our society upon the various jobs which are performed. Truly the butcher, the baker, and the candlestick maker all perform functions within our technological society upon which we all depend. The ditch digger has traditionally been relegated to one of the lowest levels of the occupational ladder, but whether he digs the ditch with a pick and shovel or with a more sophisticated backhoe, the fact remains that when we need a ditch we also need a ditch digger.

During the past decade there has been a national push for highly trained positions, particularly in the fields of mathematics and science, with little emphasis on skilled and semiskilled occupations to act as support and back-up operations. This has been particularly true in the aerospace industry, where a tremendous effort was exerted to obtain highly skilled engineers, but little emphasis was placed on the proper support teams in the form of skilled technicians. As a result, the engineers often had to leave their primary duties and attend to the straight "nuts and bolts" type operations because they did not have the support personnel who were needed. While there were warnings of our overemphasis, these warnings were largely unattended. Now, of course, we find ourselves with a shortage of workers in some of the basic services, and with at least a temporary oversupply of highly trained individuals for whom we have no work.

Dale reported on a survey of eighth grade children in the Cincinnati Public Schools asking what occupations the children planned to pursue. The results were both amusing and frightening.

What would Cincinnati be like if these 8th grade students became the sole inhabitants of the city, in the jobs of their choice, ten years from now? Health services would be very high, with every 18 people supporting one doctor. It may be, however, they would all be needed in a city that had no garbage disposal workers, no laundry workers, and no water supply, since no one chose to do that kind of work. The two bus drivers will find that their customers get tired of waiting, and use the services of the 67 airline pilots. It may be difficult getting to Crosley Field to see the 40 baseball players. (1948, p. 419)

The point of all of this, of course, is that as our society has evolved and developed, so has our interdependence upon one another for the goods and services we have come to rely upon. Gone are the days when the family was essentially self-reliant for the supply of its various needs and wants.

What then are some of the ways in which we can increase the child's awareness of the world of work? We shall very briefly consider a few in the following paragraphs.

At the turn of the century, in those families which were engaged in agriculture, the children knew very well how their parents earned their livelihood. They saw and participated in the family work alongside of their parents and siblings. By and large, today's youth lack this first-hand knowledge, because the father's and perhaps the mother's work take them outside the home. The child's understanding of the parents' work, in all probability, is quite limited in its scope. Typical responses to the question of "What does your father do?" may be vague statements

Interviewing parents

173

like, "He works in an office," "He goes to the plant," "He travels" etc. At best they are only surface responses, which demonstrate little understanding of what the parent actually does. Even children of educators are not necessarily well-informed. If one or both parents happen to be classroom teachers, the child has a clearer notion of what his parent does, but even here his view is restricted by the type of teacher to whom he has been exposed, and the degree of involvement the child has had with his teachers. The child is unlikely to have more than a vague notion of what is done by other educators. What knowledge does he have of a curriculum coordinator? A director of elementary education? A principal? A superintendent? Because the child knows the title does not mean he knows the job.

Because it is often impractical for the child to see the parent at work in his given occupation, a substitute approach which the school can employ is to have the child interview the parent about his or her job. This approach, once again, can be incorporated into the academic skills of writing and reporting.

By having the child interview his parent as completely as he can for his age, the child not only gains information about what is involved in his own parent's work, but by reporting on the results of his interview he shares this experience with his classmates, who gain equally valuable information. Care and preparation must precede the interview so that the child is able to get at the basics of the parent's occupation. Within the range of the typical classroom there should be a broad spectrum of occupations represented that will stimulate the interest of the children. In addition, if there are a few children in the class whose parents are engaged in unusual occupations, a new dimension can be added; the parents can visit the class and either tell about or demonstrate the particular occupations in which they are engaged.

How important is all of this? Apparently quite important. We can see an interesting contrast to our current American situation in an article presented by Rabkin and Rabkin (1969) dealing with life in the kibbutz. In their article they tell how children from early childhood through early adulthood are involved in the full spectrum of tasks in the kibbutz. The children also have an opportunity to see their parents, and friends of their parents, engaged in the various responsibilities of the kibbutz. By the time the children are adults, they have had exposure to nearly every aspect of the kibbutz, and the choice concerning an occupation is a relatively easy one to make. True, life in the kibbutz is far less complicated than life in industrialized America. The point is that the children of the kibbutz *know* the work of their society, while children in American society have a limited point of view. Any method we can use to expand the child's view of the world of work will make his later choices that much more sound.

Films, filmstrips, and books

Probably every experienced teacher has at least some used books or stories dealing with occupations. Fortunately, we have passed that period when there was a vague discussion of community helpers using inane and patronizing stories of our friend the policeman, the fireman, the milkman, etc. Certainly the more current materials are not only updated, but lend dignity to the various occupations discussed, as well as showing the dependence of our society upon all of these occupations.

In addition to books and stories, there are many current and well-prepared materials in the form of films, filmstrips, records, and songs which are available for classroom use. Norris (1963) has presented an excellent listing of materials and distributors of materials for school use. Other sources such as Drier (1972) and Gibson (1972) offer a variety of suggestions and examples for incorporating career development into the classroom curriculum. In addition, there are countless pamphlets available from both the private sectors of business and industry and from government—all providing information concerning various occupations which is particularly suitable for use at the upper elementary grade levels.

As with every other topic discussed in this book that has the underlying notion of promoting growth, these materials will ideally be presented in a developmental sequence from year to year. The value of any of these procedures to expose children to career possibilities will be limited if it is confined to a half-hour topic once a semester or once a year. It will also be limited if these procedures are used in a heavy dose for one school grade only. Again, the teacher is invited to make the comparison with any other academic activity to realize the importance of a continuing program of this type.

Other activities

There are a host of other activities which can be utilized in this area of understanding career development. What is presented here is not intended to be all inclusive, but suggestive instead. The teacher who knows her class well will readily think of numerous other procedures that can be employed. Some general areas for consideration follow.

Field trips. Nearly every elementary teacher has taken her class on a field trip relating to career development. Traditionally, these fall into a limited number of patterns because the children enjoy them and because the facilities are readily available. Typically the trips are confined to the supermarket, the dairy, or the bakery. There are other resources which can and should be tapped. A trip to the city incinerator or landfill, whichever the community has, provides an interesting experience for the children. In the first place, most children probably have never seen this facility and have little understanding of what happens to the trash once it leaves the home. Second, the trip will help children gain an understanding of our interdependence on each other's services. Third, the trip can be a part of class discussion of ecology, which has captured the attention and imagination of children and youth. Other destinations for trips might include: the airport, bus terminal, train depot, a light manufacturing concern, emergency facilities for the community, a farm, a sanitation plant,a water purification plant, a T.V. station, a newspaper, a social service agency, or the backstage of a professional theater.

Essays. One activity related to occupational choice that can continue throughout the elementary school is prepared and researched essays on "When I grow up I want to be_____." The essay writing can be a progressive activity determined by the skills and the level of development of the child. The essays would not only include factual material concerning occupations; they could also encourage the child to evaluate himself along as many dimensions as he can and relate all these evaluations to the abilities and skills needed for the occupation under consideration.

Team reports. Similar to the essay mentioned above, except done by groups of children organized on the basis of their particular interests, are team reports to the class on occupations, based on research and interviews. The reports could be made into a game of sorts by having a "What's My Line" panel or by giving increased bits of information to the class to see who can guess the occupations. The purpose of this activity, of course, is an ever-increasing awareness of the variety of occupations and the types of skills needed for these occupations.

Special events. The teacher, by

noting various community and state proclamations, can capitalize on them for specific discussions or reports of occupations. For example, if the mayor proclaims this "Garment Workers Week" or the governor declares it to be "Law Day," there is a timely topic—one on which the children have access to current information. The same approach could also apply to any major labor-management disputes. Again there would be readily available information.

The list of ways to familiarize children with a variety of occupations could go on. Regardless of the method used, we, as educators, have a responsibility to introduce the child to the world of work from his earliest experience in school on. The purpose is not to force earlier decisions but rather to expose the child to a broad range of information, so that when he is ready to make even a tentative choice, he has some information upon which to base it. In addition, it is critical that children have a respect and understanding for the work of others, and that they have some understanding of the contribution the whole spectrum of work makes to our health, well-being, and comfort in the twentieth century. This process is extremely important in light of the complex industrial society in which we live. It is also important that children receive not only full but unbiased information which will assist them in the exploratory process which precedes the selection of a career. This means that we make information available to all students, and that we do not impose limitations on individual students because of sex, race, or socioeconomic status. By removing these barriers we help the child begin to explore the full range of possibilities open to him or her, and by presenting a series of models, no matter how diligently we must search these models out, we help the child in his or her exploration of this full range of career possibilities.

WHAT ARE THE TEACHER'S PRIORITIES?

Much of what has been discussed in the preceding has suggested the variety of roles a teacher in the elementary school might play. It would not be unusual for many a reader to raise the question, "But how can I teach the children if I do all of this?" To a very large extent what has been suggested is teaching, but teaching at another level than that we normally consider. The extent to which what has been suggested here is in conflict with what is normally taught in the classroom is largely dependent upon the attitude and philos-

181

ophy of the teacher. In many ways we have now gone full circle back to the comments made in Chapter 1 concerning how we view the task of education and how we view the child before us.

Combs (1968) addressed himself to one of the issues involved. He stated, in effect, that we have been caught up in a fallacious, nonexistent dichotomy believing that somehow we have to make a choice between educating children to become smart and disturbed, or dumb and well adjusted. We tend to believe that the teacher must decide whether to educate the cognitive or the affective side of the child. Combs feels the choice is a futile one, based on an artificial separation. We cannot deal with only one side of a child or the other. When we deal with the cognitive side, we must likewise deal with the affective, and vice versa.

Montagu (1970) has also spoken to much the same issue when he raised the question of what education really means. He suggests that much of education today is a ritualistic process of piling fact after fact upon the child with little or no regard for the child as an individual. He suggests instead that education should be a relationship between child and teacher, based on love and respect for the individual, where the final outcome is a mutual process of exploring and searching for a meaning for life.

Perhaps all of this sounds overdrawn, idealistic, and maybe a bit too sentimental. After all, there are lesson plans and curriculum guides to be met. There are many who would contend that this is the real stuff of education. Perhaps so, but does this necessarily preclude a respect, understanding, and caring for the child as an individual? Both have a place in the over-all process of education.

What are these demands in caring for the child? Many teachers maintain they do care for children or they would not be teaching, but is this always an adequate demonstration of concern? Do effective parents feel that because they have produced a child they have given an adequate demonstration of love and caring for their child? Hardly.

We all need periodic reassurance of the concern of others for us. Quite typically, these demonstrations are small, but meaningful, gestures which require so little to give, but which mean so much to the person receiving them.

An example may be helpful. Following is part of a letter from a parent in response to a teacher who took the time to call the parents to share her concern for their child.

Dear Mrs.———

I'm an emotional sentimentalist; this may help you understand how deeply I was touched by your kind act of calling to explain to us your own and Joan's distress over the issuance of the progress notice.

Being emotional and sentimental, it's not hard for me to have intense feelings over the trend toward greater efficiency in our school systems. I'm the kind of person who believes it to be a retreat when the family doctor introduces an IBM billing and diagnostic system into his office. I see the replacement of the corner grocery with the 7–11 and the "super" market as retrogression; and I see the increase in statisticians, mergers, controller-run businesses and public authorities, forms, psychological testing as not really worthy of the worship we are asked to give them.

Consequently, I'm disrespectful of printed notices of all kinds, and especially toward those directed to the Joaneys in the student world. These, the notices, are most successful in bringing my bias to the fore. They arouse my passion. They increase my skepticism—they force me to be a heretic, and I refuse to consider the efficiency they promise as just compensation for the terror and dehumanizing they introduce.

Mrs. _____, a Joaney will have received many progress notices by the time she has reached 8th grade. . . . You would be amazed at the consistency in the evaluations. It is almost as though there was collusion—the system vs. the Joans. If you, dedicated, concerned as you are (and your call to us is proof enough of that), were to accumulate a random sampling of these notices (they used to be called warnings) you would have to conclude, I believe, that the problem doesn't lie entirely with Joaneys, but from the evidence, lies partly with the system. . . .

Please be tolerant with me. I am in no way being critical of you. My appraisal of you after visiting the school was that you were a "chip" among teachers. And, as a "chip" you have the capacity to be a miracle-producing agent for those you touch. Your call, your involvement with the person who is Joan, offers evidence of an even greater capacity; the capacity of awareness, the capacity of love, if you will— the capacity of doing to and for others what you would wish to be done to and for yourself. Greater love than this no teacher can have for a student.

In my opinion, and this too is a bias, you could not direct that love to one more deserving than Joan. For, in my opinion, she's a Billy Budd among us for she loves in a superior way too, so much so, that if the teaching staff exposed to Joan was united in common purpose to lead Joaney to the joy of learning, they would be doing no more than repaying her for the ready smile, the constant affection she's ever-ready to shower freely on anyone in need of it.

Thank you again, Mrs. _____. I am more grateful than my capacity for expression.

(McGirr, 1968)

Shane (1961) and others cautioned us a decade ago that the increasing class sizes would at the least have the tendency to separate the teacher from the class to the point the teacher would not know the students as well and, therefore, would not offer the children the individual attention they needed. These predictions, unfortunately, have been borne out.

During the last decade there was a movement afoot for education to become more efficient and the business world

186

model was advocated. (Though after reading Peter and Hull's *The Peter Principle* [1969], one might question this choice of a model.) In any event, it was common to hear educators raising the question, "If this practice were followed in business, how long would they stay in business?" Those who wanted to use the business model believed that if the whole operation were made more efficient children would learn more effectively. If the model of business is to be used for the operation of the school, we should first of all give attention to one of the most dramatic lessons business and industry have learned, the result of the now famous Hawthorne study some thirty years ago. (Mayo, 1945) The Hawthorne plant is located outside of Chicago, and at the time of the study its management wanted to determine what could be done to increase the efficiency of the workers. After some deliberation it was decided to improve the lighting in a selected area of the plant. The lighting was improved, observations were made, and production increased. Following the maxim that if a little is good, more is better, once again the lighting was increased, observations were made, and production increased. After several experiments in this same direction, each with increased production, someone raised the question of what would happen if the lighting were diminished. In order to answer this the lighting was changed again, but with a reduction rather than an increase. Again observations were made and production continued to climb. The lighting was progressively decreased until the work area was described as being no brighter than a bright moonlight night. When the observations were made this time the high production rate was maintained. After extended evaluation and analysis of this situation, the final conclusion was that the workers were responding not to the physical changes in their working conditions *per se*, but to the interest being shown in them. The workers were more satisfied, more productive, and more efficient because management was showing an interest in the worker's welfare.

Children in their play activities often imitate adult behavior. These caricatures are often funny, often exaggerated as the child attempts to act in adultlike manner, and often present the harsh perceptions of the child as he views adult behavior. Perhaps from the poetry of a child we may see at least one young child's perception of education and the teacher:

I want to be a teacher when I grow up
then I can write on the marking board

and I can pull kids' ears
put them in the closet
punch and shake them till they cry
and I can smack them

(Dooley, 1968, p. 16)

What then should be the role of the teacher? There is a great deal to suggest that the truly effective teacher is a partner in learning with the child. She is a participant with the child in discovering the joy and meaning of the child's life. She develops a continued awareness of and sensitivity to the child.

Combs (1961) stated the need for sensitivity forcefully, with his penetrating comments:

We need to develop a sensitivity to how things seem to the people with whom we are working. For a long time we have advocated in teacher-training institutions the idea that teachers need to understand the child. What has often happened, however, is that we have confused understanding *about* a child with understanding the child *himself.* Even when I know a great deal about human growth and development, I may fail to understand a given child. When I have made a careful study of him, when I have interviewed his parents, searched

189

his school records, looked over his health and physical records, tested and examined him fore and aft, I still may not understand him. I do not really understand him until I have learned to see how he sees himself, and how he sees the world in which he lives. All of this information about him will be of limited value until I have come to understand the way he sees things in his private world of meaning and feeling. There is a world of difference between understanding a *person*, and understanding *about* him.

The kind of understanding we are talking about here is not a *knowledge about*, but a *sensitivity* to people. It is a kind of empathy, the ability to put oneself in another's shoes, to feel and see as he does. All of us have this ability to some extent, but good teachers have a lot of it. (p. 19)

SOME CONCLUDING CONSIDERATIONS

We have now gone full circle in our discussion of elementary guidance and the elementary teacher. The guidance function performed by the teacher in the elementary school is first and foremost an attitude: an attitude of respect, understanding, and caring for children committed to the teacher's care.

From this attitude will spring a number of practices aimed at facilitating the full growth and development of the child. The practices suggested in this book are not complete, nor are they guaranteed to bring quick and lasting results. The teacher who knows and understands the children in her class will also be innovative and will go far beyond the few suggestions presented here.

Haimowitz (1966) reacted to the importance of attitude forcefully and effectively in his article, "What Kind of People Do We Want?", part of which follows:

... Men at all times have sought truth, beauty, and justice, but they have rarely agreed on what these are. Each generation learns the values of its fathers and then rebels against them. In one generation, firm discipline is advocated, but in the next, a thousand reasons are manufactured for sparing the rod. Should we be governed by fashion in such matters? Or is there some objective way to establish an optimal climate for a favorable human condition?

What do we want in life? What do we want for our children? If it is pleasure we seek, why do we work so hard? If "freedom," then, specifically, freedom from what and to do what? Courage to risk our lives on the battle-field or courage to refuse to do battle; courage to submit or courage to rebel? Wealth might be the goal, but it often appears that the rich are slaves to their riches. Or perhaps we desire to love our neighbors as ourselves; child sacrifice is not advocated, but we manage—in a land overflowing with milk and honey —to sacrifice many of our neighbor's children to poverty, ignorance, disease, pollution, unemployment,and drugs . . .*

*From *Human Development: Selected Readings* by Morris L. Haimowitz and Natalie Reader Haimowitz. Copyright©1973 by Thomas Y. Crowell Company, Inc., with permission of the publisher.

What kind of people do we want? What kind of people do *you* want? From all that has preceded the notion that prevails is the teacher's power of humaneness in the learning and growing process of the child. There are many who contend that when all the unimportant dates and facts have been forgotten by the learner, the most significant memory which remains is the quality of the child's interaction with the teacher. Perhaps it is the learning that stems from this interaction which is the most important learning, after all, and from it the learning of skills and facts cannot only take place, but also take on the significance needed to move and direct the life of the child.

References

CHAPTER 1

Burnham, W. *The Wholesome Personality*. New York: D. Appleton Company, 1926.

Combs, A. H. "What can man become?" Paper presented in the Great Speakers Series, Pennsylvania Department of Education, Harrisburg, Pennsylvania, 1968.

Faust, V. E. *History of Elementary School Counseling: Overview and Critique*. Boston: Houghton-Mifflin, 1968.

Haimowitz, M. L., and Haimowitz, N. R. *Human Development: Selected Readings*. New York: Thomas Y. Crowell Company, 1966.

CHAPTER 2

Burack, B. "Have You Checked Machine-Scoring Error?" *The Vocational Guidance Quarterly* 9: 191–93, Spring 1961.

Buros, O. K., ed. *Mental Measurement Yearbook.* Highland Park, New Jersey: Gryphon Press, 1969.

———. *Tests in Print.* Highland Park, New Jersey: Gryphon Press, 1961.

Cronbach, L. *Essentials of Psychological Testing.* New York: Harper and Row, 1970.

Fenner, M. S., ed. "A Briefing for Parents: Your Child's Intelligence." *N.E.A. Journal* 50: 33–43, January 1961.

Goldman, L. *Using Tests in Counseling.* New York: Appleton-Century-Crofts, 1961.

Goodenough, F. L. *Mental Testing.* New York: Rinehart and Company, Inc., 1950.

Goslin, D. A., conference chairman. "Guidelines for the Collection, Maintenance, and Dissemination of Pupil Records." Sterling Forest, New York: Russell Sage Foundation, 1969.

Hoffmann, B. *The Tyranny of Testing.* New York: The Crowell-Collier Press, 1962.

Kagan, J., and Moss, H. *Birth to Maturity: A Study in Psychological Development.* New York: John Wiley and Sons, 1962.

Merwin, J. C.; Bradley, A. D.; Johnson, R. H.; and John, E. R. "S.V.I.B. Machine Scoring Provided by a Test Scoring Agency." *Personnel and Guidance Journal* 43: 665–68, March 1965.

Rosenthal, R., and Jacobson, L. *Pygmalion in the Classroom.* New York: Holt, Rinehart and Winston, Inc., 1968.

Seashore, H., ed. *Test Service Bulletin.* #54. New York: Psychological Corporation, 1959.

Super, D., and Crites, J. *Appraising Vocational Fitness.* New York: Harper and Row, 1962.

Tyler, L. *Tests and Measurements.* Englewood Cliffs, New Jersey: Prentice-Hall, Inc., 1963.

Weigel, R.; Roehlke, A.; and Poe, C. "Re-evaluating Machine Scoring Consistency." *The Vocational Guidance Quarterly* 13: 209–11, Spring 1965.

CHAPTER 3

Bamman, H. A., and Whitehead, R. J. *The Checkered Flag Series.* San Francisco: Harr Wagner Publishing Company, 1968.

References

Bolig, J. R. Sex Segregated Kindergartens as a Means of Reducing the Number of Problems Children Encounter in School. unpublished doctoral dissertation, Lehigh University, 1971.

Brookover, W. B. Self-concept and achievement. Paper presented at American Educational Convention, Los Angeles, February, 1969.

Brookover, W. B.; Erickson, E. L.; and Joiner, L. M. Self-concept of ability and school achievement. The Relationship of self-concept to achievement in high school. U.S.O.E., Cooperative Research Project No. 2831. East Lansing: Office of Research and Publications, Michigan State University, 1967.

Combs, A. W. "Curriculum Change and the Humanist Movement." *Educational Leadership* 23: 527–30, April 1966.

_____. "What Can Man Become?" Great Speakers Series, Department of Public Instruction, Harrisburg, Pennsylvania, 1968.

Coopersmith, S. *The Antecedents of Self-esteem.* San Francisco: W. H. Freeman and Company, 1967.

Curtis, O. "All-Male Classroom." *Philadelphia Inquirer Magazine,* May 26, 1968, p. 20–21.

Davidson, H. H., and Greenberg, J. W. School achievers from a deprived background. U.S.O.E. Project No. 2805, Contract No. OE-5-10-132. New York: The City College of the City University of New York, 1967.

Davis, A. *Social-Class Influence Upon Learning*. Cambridge, Massachusetts; Harvard University Press, 1948.

Dittes, J. E. Effects of changes in self-esteem upon impulsiveness and deliberation in making judgments. *Journal of Abnormal and Social Psychology* 58: 348–56, 1959.

Dolan, V. "Stag Kindergarten," *Look* 33: 21, 103–4, October 21, 1969.

Fromm, E. *Escape from Freedom*. New York: Holt, Rinehart and Winston, Inc., 1941.

_____. *Man for himself*. New York: Holt, Rinehart and Winston, Inc., 1947.

Getzels, J. W., and Jackson, P. W. *Creativity and Intelligence*. New York: John Wiley and Sons, 1962.

Goodenough, F. L. *Mental Testing*. New York: Rinehart and Company, Inc., 1950.

Havighurst, R.; Bowman, F.; Liddle, G.; Matthews, C.; and Pierce, J. *Growing Up in River City*. New York: John Wiley and Sons, 1962.

Hollingshead, A. *Elmtown's Youth*. New

References

York: John Wiley and Sons, 1949.

Jencks, C., et al. *Inequality: A Reassessment of the Effect of Family and Schooling in America.* New York: Basic Books, Inc., 1972.

Kagan, J. "The Child's Perception of the Parent." *Journal of Abnormal Social Psychology* 53: 257, 1956.

_____. "The Child's Sex Role Classification of School Objects." *Child Development* 35: 1051, 1964.

_____. "The Theoretical Foundations of Psychological Development in the Early School Years." *Elementary School Guidance Work Conference,* Pennsylvania Department of Public Instruction, 1969.

Kagan, J.; Hoskin, B.; and Watson, S. "The Child's Symbolic Conceptualization of the Parents." *Child Development* 32: 625, 1961.

McCandless, B. R. *Children: Behavior and Development.* New York: Holt, Rinehart and Winston, Inc., 1967.

Olson, W. C., and Hughes, B. O. "Concepts of Growth—Their Significance to Teachers." *Childhood Education* 21: 53–63, October 1944.

Pollack, J. H. "Are Teachers Fair to Boys?" *Today's Health,* April 1968, p. 21–25.

Purkey, W. W. *Self Concept and School Achievement.* Englewood Cliffs, New Jersey: Prentice-Hall, 1970.

Rosenthal, R., and Jacobson, L. *Pygmalion in the Classroom.* New York: Holt, Rinehart and Winston, Inc., 1968.

Ringness, T. A. Self-concept of children of low, average, and high intelligence. *American Journal of Mental Deficiency* 65: 453–61, 1961.

Sexton, P., "How the American Boy is Feminized." *Psychology Today* 3: 23–29, 66–67, January 1970.

Skinner, B. F. *Beyond Freedom and Dignity.* New York: Alfred A. Knopf, 1971.

_____. *The Technology of Teaching.* New York: Appleton-Century-Crofts, 1968.

_____. *Walden Two.* New York: The Macmillan Co., 1948.

Strickler, R. W., and Phillips, C. M. "Kindergarten Success Story." *Instructor,* December 1970, p. 49–51.

Taylor, R. G. Personality traits and discrepant achievement: A review. *Journal of Counseling Psychology* 11: 76–81, 1964.

CHAPTER 4

Arbuckle, D. S. "Occupational Information in the Elementary School." *The Vocational Guidance Quarterly* 12: 77–84, Winter 1964.

Barbe, W. B., and Chambers, N. S. "Career

Requirements of Gifted Elementary Children and Their Parents." *The Vocational Guidance Quarterly* 11: 137–40, Winter 1963.

Combs, A. H. "What Can Man Become?" *California Journal for Instructional Improvement* 4: 15–23, 1961.

_____. "What Can Man Become?" Great Speakers Series, Department of Public Instruction, Harrisburg, Pennsylvania, 1968.

Dale, R. V. H. "To Youth Who Choose Blindly." *Occupations*, April 1948, p. 419.

Dooley, S., ed. *Vista Volunteer.* Office of Economic Opportunity, Washington, D. C. 4: 4, April 1968.

Drier, H. N., Jr. *K–12 Guide for Integrating Career Development into Local Curriculum.* Worthington, Ohio: Charles A. Jones Publishing Company, 1972.

Gibson, R. L. *Career Development in the Elementary School.* Columbus, Ohio: Charles E. Merril Publishing Company, 1972.

Ginzberg, E.; Ginsburg, S. W.; Axlerad, S.; and Herma, J. L. *Occupational Choices: An Approach to a General Theory.* New York: Columbia University Press, 1951.

Grell, L. A. "How Much Occupational

Information in the Elementary
School?" *The Vocational Guidance
Quarterly* 9: 48–53, Autumn 1960.

Haimowitz, M. L., and Haimowitz, N. R.
*Human Development: Selected
Readings.* New York: Thomas Y.
Crowell Company, 1966.

Holland, J. L. "A Theory of Vocational
Choice." *Journal of Counseling
Psychology* 6: 35–44, 1959.

Hoppock, R. *Occupational Information.*
New York: McGraw-Hill, 1957.

———. *Occupational Information.* New
York: McGraw-Hill, 1967.

Kaback, G. R. "Automation, Work and
Leisure: Implications for Elementary
Education." *The Vocational Guidance
Quarterly* 13: 202–6, Spring 1967.

———. "Occupational Information in
Elementary Education." *The
Vocational Guidance Quarterly* 9: 55–
59, Autumn 1960.

———. "Occupational Information for
Groups of Elementary School
Children." *The Vocational Guidance
Quarterly* 4: 163–68, Spring 1966.

Kaye, J. "Fourth Graders Meet Up with
Occupations." *The Vocational
Guidance Quarterly* 8: 150–52, Spring
1960.

Kranzler, G. D.; Mayer, R.; Dyer, C. O.; and
Munger, P. F. "Counseling with

Elementary School Children: An Experimental Study." *Personnel and Guidance Journal* 44: 944–49, May 1966.

Limbacher, W. J. *Dimensions of Personality.* Dayton, Ohio: George A. Pflaum, 1970.

Lippman, H. S. *Treatment of the Child in Emotional Conflict.* New York: McGraw-Hill Book Company, 1962.

McGirr, A. J. Unpublished correspondence, 1968.

Mayo, E. *The Social Problems of an Industrialized Civilization.* New York: Andover Press, 1945.

Montagu, A. "A Scientist Looks at Love." *Phi Delta Kappan* 51: 463–67, May 1970.

Morse, W. C. "Training Teachers in Life Space Interviewing." *American Journal of Orthopsychiatry* 33: 727–30, July 1963.

Moustakas, C. E. "Conflict with A Pupil." *N.E.A. Journal* 50: 54, January 1961.

Myers, D. G. *A Comparison of the Effects of Group Puppet Therapy and Group Activity with Mentally Retarded Children.* Unpublished doctoral dissertation, Lehigh University, 1970.

National Education Association. *More Unfinished Stories for Use in the Classroom.* Washington, D. C.:

National Education Association, 1971.

Nelson, R. C. "Early Versus Developmental Vocational Choice." *The Vocational Guidance Quarterly* 11: 23–27, Autumn 1962.

Norris, W. *Occupational Information in the Elementary School*. Chicago: Science Research Associates, Inc., 1963.

Ohlsen, M. M. *Guidance Services in the Modern School*. New York: Harcourt, Brace and World, 1964.

Ojemann, R. *A Teaching Program in Human Behavior and Mental Health*. Cleveland: The Educational Research Council of Greater Cleveland, 1964.

Parsons, F. *Choosing a Vocation*. Boston: Houghton Mifflin, 1909.

Peter, L. J., and Hull, R. *The Peter Principle*. New York: William Morrow and Company, 1969.

Rabkin, L. Y., and Rabkin, K. "Children of the Kibbutz." *Psychology Today* 3: 40–46, September 1969.

Roe, A. *The Psychology of Occupations*. New York: John Wiley and Sons, 1956.

Shane, H. G. "Class Size and Human Development." *N.E.A. Journal* 50: 30–32, January 1961.

Super, D. E. *The Psychology of Careers*. New York: Harper and Brothers, 1957.

References

Super, D. E., et al. *Vocational Development: A Framework for Research.* New York: Teachers College, Columbia University, 1957.

Tennyson, W. W., and Monnens, L. P. "The World of Work Through Elementary Readers." *The Vocational Guidance Quarterly* 12: 85–88, Winter 1964.

Thompson, E., ed. *Unfinished Stories for the Classroom.* Washington, D. C.: National Education Association for the United States of America, 1966.

Name Index

J–K

L

M

N

O

P–Q

Subject index

Abuse of testing, 75–76
Accountability
  students, 100
  teachers, 101
Achievement, 91*ff.*
  social influences, 110*ff.*
Administrator, educational, 106–7
Anxiety of failure, 133–34
Attitudes, 137*ff.*
  students, 86*ff.*, 115–16, 147
  teachers, 84*ff.*, 115–16

Behavior change, 143*ff.*
  learning, 139*ff.*
Behavioral theory, 108–9
Boys and girls, 124*ff.*

A

B

V–W